Lecture Notes in Computer Science 14677

Founding Editors

Gerhard Goos
Juris Hartmanis

The series Lecture Notes in Computer Science (LNCS), including its subseries Lecture Notes in Artificial Intelligence (LNAI) and Lecture Notes in Bioinformatics (LNBI), has established itself as a medium for the publication of new developments in computer science and information technology research, teaching, and education.

LNCS enjoys close cooperation with the computer science R & D community, the series counts many renowned academics among its volume editors and paper authors, and collaborates with prestigious societies. Its mission is to serve this international community by providing an invaluable service, mainly focused on the publication of conference and workshop proceedings and postproceedings. LNCS commenced publication in 1973.

Rolando Martins · Mennan Selimi
Editors

Distributed Applications and Interoperable Systems

24th IFIP WG 6.1 International Conference, DAIS 2024
Held as Part of the 19th International Federated Conference
on Distributed Computing Techniques, DisCoTec 2024
Groningen, The Netherlands, June 17–21, 2024
Proceedings

 Springer

Editors
Rolando Martins (iD)
University of Porto
Porto, Portugal

Mennan Selimi
South East European University
Tetovo, North Macedonia

ISSN 0302-9743   ISSN 1611-3349 (electronic)
Lecture Notes in Computer Science
ISBN 978-3-031-62637-1   ISBN 978-3-031-62638-8 (eBook)
https://doi.org/10.1007/978-3-031-62638-8

This Springer imprint is published by the registered company Springer Nature Switzerland AG
The registered company address is: Gewerbestrasse 11, 6330 Cham, Switzerland

If disposing of this product, please recycle the paper.

Foreword

The 19th International Federated Conference on Distributed Computing Techniques (DisCoTec) took place in Groningen, The Netherlands, during June 17–21, 2024. It was organized by the Bernoulli Institute of Mathematics, Computer Science, and Artificial Intelligence at the University of Groningen, The Netherlands.

The DisCoTec series is one of the major events sponsored by the International Federation for Information Processing (IFIP). It comprises three main conferences:

- COORDINATION, the IFIP WG6.1 26th International Conference on Coordination Models and Languages – Program Chairs: Ilaria Castellani (Inria Sophia Antipolis, France) and Francesco Tiezzi (University of Florence, Italy).
- DAIS, the IFIP WG6.1 24th International Conference on Distributed Applications and Interoperable Systems – Program Chairs: Rolando Martins (University of Porto, Portugal) and Mennan Selimi (South East European University, North Macedonia).
- FORTE, the IFIP WG6.1 44th International Conference on Formal Techniques for Distributed Objects, Components and Systems – Program Chairs: Valentina Castiglioni (Eindhoven University of Technology, The Netherlands) and Adrian Francalanza (University of Malta, Malta).

Together, these conferences cover a broad spectrum of distributed computing subjects—from theoretical foundations and formal description techniques, testing and verification methods, to language design and system implementation approaches.

Following recent developments in the research community, all conferences included an Artifact Evaluation track, whose goal is to improve and reward research reproducibility and to increase visibility of the effort of tool developers. Each conference implemented this track independently, in close coordination with Roberto Casadei (University of Bologna, Italy) who served as Artifact Evaluation chair.

In addition to the individual sessions of each conference, the event included several plenary sessions that gathered attendants from the three conferences. In coordination with the General Chair, the three DisCoTec conferences selected the plenary keynote speakers. The three keynote speakers and the title of their talks is listed below:

- Prof. Laura Kovács (Vienna University of Technology, Austria) – *Automated Reasoning in BlockChain Security*
- Prof. Paulo Veríssimo (KAUST, CEMSE, RC3 - Resilient Computing and Cyber-security Center, Saudi Arabia) – *Platform Resilience? Beware of Threats from the "basement"*
- Prof. Marieke Huisman (University of Twente, The Netherlands) – *VerCors: Inclusive Software Verification*

As traditional in DisCoTec, the program included an additional joint session with the best papers from each conference. The best papers were:

- *A Probabilistic Choreography Language for PRISM*, by Marco Carbone and Adele Veschetti;
- *Compact Storage of Data Streams in Mobile Devices*, by Rémy Raes, Olivier Ruas, Adrien Luxey-Bitri, Romain Rouvoy;
- *Weak Simplicial Bisimilarity for Polyhedral Models and SLCSη*, by Nick Bezhanishvili, Vincenzo Ciancia, David Gabelaia, Mamuka Jibladze, Diego Latella, Mieke Massink and Erik De Vink.

The federated event was further enriched with the following three satellite events:

- DiDiT: The 1st International Workshop on Distributed Digital Twins, organized by Victoria Degeler (University of Amsterdam, The Netherlands), Dilek Dustegor (University of Groningen, The Netherlands), Heerko Groefsema (University of Groningen, The Netherlands), and Elena Lazovik (TNO, The Netherlands).
- ICE: 17th Interaction and Concurrency Experience, organized by Clément Aubert (Augusta University, USA), Cinzia Di Giusto (Université Côte d'Azur, France), Simon Fowler (University of Glasgow, UK), and Violet Ka I Pun (Western Norway University of Applied Sciences, Norway).
- PLNL: The Fourth Workshop on Programming Languages in The Netherlands, organized by Daniel Frumin (University of Groningen, The Netherlands) and Wouter Swierstra (Utrecht University, Netherlands) on behalf of VERSEN, the Dutch National Association for Software Engineering.

I would like to thank the Program Committee chairs of the different events for their cooperation during the preparation of the federated event, the Artifact Evaluation chair for his dedicated coordination work, and the Steering Committee of DisCoTec and their conferences for their guidance and support. Moreover, I am grateful to the keynote speakers and all conference attendees for joining us in Groningen.

The organization of DisCoTec 2024 was only possible thanks to the hard work and dedication of the Organizing Committee, including Bas van den Heuvel (publicity chair), Daniel Frumin and Claudio Antares Mezzina (workshop co-chairs), Magda Piekorz and Ineke Schelhaas (logistics and finances), as well as all the colleagues and students who volunteered their time to help.

Finally, I would like to thank IFIP WG6.1 for sponsoring this event, Springer's Lecture Notes in Computer Science team for their support and sponsorship, EasyChair for providing the reviewing infrastructure, the Dutch Research Council (NWO) for financial support (file number 21382), and the Faculty of Science and Engineering of the University of Groningen for providing meeting rooms and administrative support.

June 2024   Jorge A. Pérez

Preface

This volume contains the papers presented at the 24rd IFIP International Conference on Distributed Applications and Interoperable Systems (DAIS 2024), sponsored by the International Federation for Information Processing (IFIP) and organized by IFIP WG 6.1. The DAIS conference series addresses all practical and conceptual aspects of distributed applications, including their design, modeling, implementation, and operation; the supporting middleware; appropriate software engineering methodologies and tools; and experimental studies and applications. DAIS 2024 was held during June 17–21, 2024, in Groningen, The Netherlands, as part of DisCoTec 2024, the 19th International Federated Conference on Distributed Computing Techniques.

We offered three distinct paper tracks: full research papers, full practical experience reports, and work-in-progress papers. We received 17 submissions, where 16 were full papers and 1 was a short paper. All submissions were single-blind reviewed by nearly four Program Committee (PC) members. The review process included a post-review discussion phase, during which the merits of all papers were discussed by the PC. The committee decided to accept five full research papers, for an acceptance rate of 29%. The accepted papers cover a broad range of topics in distributed computing: edge computing, data storage, data streaming and cryptocurrency analysis.

This year, we also decided to invite authors of accepted papers to submit publicly available artifacts associated with their papers. This process was chaired by João Soares and Nuhi Besimi. We unfortunately did not received any artifacts.

The keynote for DAIS was presented by distinguished lecturer Prof. Paulo Veríssimo, who is currently the Director of the Resilient Computing and Cybersecurity Center (RC3) at King Abdullah University of Science and Technology (KAUST). The keynote, titled "Platform Resilience? Beware of Threats from the 'basement'", featured the following abstract:

"Modern distributed and/or modular computer systems rely on support abstractions to ease the task of building applications, such as middleware, hypervisors, libraries of secure or fault-tolerant functions, specialized hardware extensions, etc.

Over the years, given the undeniable successes of these abstractions, there has been a tendency to overestimate their reliability. For example, considering that complex middleware can be made fault free, or assuming that a hypervisor is a TCB. Such threats coming "from the basement" (since they were not assumed) can lead to unexpected and severe failures. What has been done about this, and what more can we do? I will digress through several approaches aiming at achieving sufficient resilience of platforms at several levels, namely middleware and hypervisor fault and intrusion tolerance. But this is not enough. As years go by, threats appear at progressively lower levels. I will report some recent results aiming at achieving resilience at quite low levels of platform architectures, such as MPSoC (multi-processor systems-on-a-chip) and FPGA fabrics, exemplifying how these mechanisms yield resilience at the higher levels of modular and distributed systems."

The conference was made possible by the hard work and cooperation of many people working in several different committees and organizations, all of which are listed in these proceedings. In particular, we are grateful to the PC members for their commitment and thorough reviews, and for their active participation in the discussion phase, and to all the external reviewers for their help in evaluating submissions. We are also grateful to the AEC members for their availability. Finally, we also thank the DisCoTec General Chair, Jorge Pérez, the DAIS Steering Committee Chair, Luís Veiga, and last year's DAIS PC Chair João Paulo, for their constant availability, support, and guidance.

June 2024

Rolando Martins
Mennan Selimi

Organization

Program Committee

Pierre-Louis Aublin	IIJ Research Laboratory, Japan
Paolo Bellavista	University of Bologna, Italy
David Bermbach	TU Berlin, Germany
Nuhi Besimi	South East European University, North Macedonia
Fred Buining	HIRO-MicroDataCenters BV, The Netherlands
Zhiyuan Chen	University of Maryland Baltimore County, USA
Håvard Dagenborg	UiT – The Arctic University of Norway, Norway
Kalyvianaki Evangelia	University of Cambridge, UK
Felix Freitag	Universitat Politècnica de Catalunya, Spain
Davide Frey	Inria, France
Rüdiger Kapitza	FAU Erlangen-Nürnberg, Germany
Pradeeban Kathiravelu	University of Alaska, Anchorage, USA
João Leitão	NOVA LINCS, DI-FCT–UNL, Portugal
Odorico Mendizabal	Universidade Federal de Santa Catarina, Brazil
Carlos Molina	University of Cambridge, UK
Guillaume Pierre	University of Rennes, Inria, CNRS, IRISA, France
Kai Rannenberg	Goethe University Frankfurt, Germany
Hans Reiser	Reykjavik University, Iceland
Mirela Riveni	TU Wien, Austria
Etienne Riviére	Université catholique de Louvain, Belgium
Valerio Schiavoni	University of Neuchâtel, Switzerland
Ali Shoker	KAUST, Saudi Arabia
João Soares	University of Porto, Portugal
Luis Veiga	INESC-ID, University of Lisbon, Portugal
Spyros Voulgaris	Vrije Universiteit Amsterdam, The Netherlands
Roberto Yus	University of Maryland, Baltimore County, USA
Marco Zennaro	Abdus Salam International Centre for Theoretical Physics, Italy

Contents

Stream Economics: Resource Efficiency in Streams with Task Over-Allocation and Load Shedding

Luís Alves[1,2] and Luís Veiga[1,2(✉)]

[1] INESC-ID Lisboa, Lisboa, Portugal
luis.veiga@inesc-id.pt
[2] Instituto Superior Técnico, Universidade de Lisboa, Lisboa, Portugal

Abstract. In this paper we propose an alternative task scheduling mechanism for stream processing systems such as Apache Flink, that targets resource efficiency in a multi-tenant stream processing environment with several resource heterogeneous tasks being executed in parallel. The task scheduler we propose doesn't limit the amount of tasks that can run on each machine, instead, it adapts tasks' allocation based on their runtime metrics, scheduling tasks to the machines with more available resources. At the same time, we explore load shedding in stream processing applications, as a mechanism to solve the tasks' resource starvation problem that may appear due to bad decisions performed by the scheduler, because of its optimistic approach and due to the dynamic workloads of the applications. We implemented a proof-of-concept of such system in Apache Flink and tested it against scenarios that show the different aspects and advantages of the developed mechanism in action.

1 Introduction

Efficient resource management in environments where several heterogeneous applications are executed has shown to be a challenging problem. In such environments, it is common to observe situations of resource underutilization, which happens because resources tend to be provisioned to the peak workload. While on average workloads, these provisioned resources are not fully utilized [11], leading to unnecessary costs and energy waste. In fact, estimations can be found, claiming below 60% resource utilization on datacenters [19].

Overallocation of tasks to resources, appears as a clear solution to handle this problem [6]. Nonetheless, it yields another problem, since resource underprovisioning situations can occur, having an impact on the applications' performance. This causes the need to monitor the applications' runtime execution to detect these situations; and to have a compensation mechanism that guarantees that the SLAs keep being fulfilled while resource wastage is avoided, such as

---

L. Alves—Work carried out in the context of MSc thesis while at[1,2].

Published by Springer Nature Switzerland AG 2024
R. Martins and M. Selimi (Eds.): DAIS 2024, LNCS 14677, pp. 1–17, 2024.
https://doi.org/10.1007/978-3-031-62638-8_1

auto-scaling [20]. Additionally, resource estimation models have also been subject of study, allowing to reduce the need of this compensation mechanism [17].

In this paper, we focus on exploring both these problems applied to the domain of distributed stream processing systems, such as Apache Flink [2,7]. Our solution consists in a task scheduling policy that assigns tasks to the machines with more available resources, in terms of CPU usage. Thus, avoiding resource overallocation by simply dropping the concept of resource reservation.

Nonetheless, it may lead to situations of resource starvation. When such situations are detected, two possible approaches are proposed. The system can either decide to perform *Task Re-scheduling* of specific tasks to other machines, causing application downtime; or to use *Load Shedding*, allowing applications to keep up with their incoming workload at the cost of decreasing the accuracy of their results. This second approach is preferred, only using the first one as a last resource.

To guide the system decisions, two restrictions can be specified by the user, for each application's queries: their *priority*, which allows users to define some queries as being more important than others; and their *minimum acceptable accuracy*. This last restriction is relevant, since below a given accuracy, the results provided by a query stop being useful or even meaningful to the user. Both these restrictions are crucial for the system to decide when to use *Load Shedding*; and when to switch to *Task Re-scheduling*. This, as well as on deciding on which tasks these mechanisms should be triggered, clearly being the low priority tasks the first ones to be targeted.

As such, the main contribution from this paper consists in a novel resource management model, for stream processing systems, that uses both dynamic task scheduling and load shedding. Obtained results show improvements on resource efficiency and on the applications' latency and throughput in bottleneck situations.

This paper is organized as follows: Sect. 2 provides a background and an overview of the solution's architecture; Sect. 3 presents the model that governs the system's decisions; Sect. 4 details the system components and their underlying algorithms; Sect. 5 shows the evaluation of the developed proof-of-concept; and Sect. 6 focuses on related work. Finally, Sect. 7 wraps up some conclusions as well as future directions.

2   Architecture

Although the solution developed in this paper can be generalized to other distributed stream processing systems, our architecture specifically targets Apache Flink [2,7], a modern instance of such systems that will allow us to demonstrate our proposed mechanism. Flink's architecture is organized in three main components: the JM, receives requests to deploy applications, schedules their tasks and monitors their execution; the TM that execute the actual tasks on the slots that they provide to the cluster; and the *Client*, that compiles the application dataflow and sends it to the JM for execution.

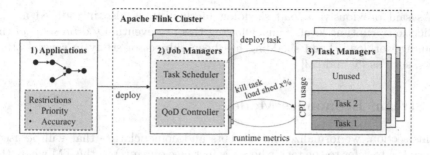

Fig. 1. Architecture and components of the proposed system in a Flink cluster.

A Flink application is modeled as a DAG, where the nodes represent operators that perform computations on the tuples they receive; these nodes are linked via streams that connect the output of one operator with the input of another. Nodes without upstream nodes are named *sources*, while nodes without downstream nodes are named *sinks* or *queries*. At runtime an operator can have several parallel running instances, named *sub-tasks*. A chain of sub-tasks can be grouped into a single *task*, which is executed by a single thread, where the sub-tasks perform computations sequentially on the received events. For higher throughput, Flink allows to pipeline sub-tasks, i.e. split a chain of sub-tasks into multiple tasks being executed by separated threads in parallel.

Figure 1 presents a bird's eye view of the previously described Flink components together with two key components introduced by our solution: the new *Task Scheduler*, that schedules tasks over the available TM by following the already described policy; and the *Quality-of-Data Controller (QoD Controller)* that constantly monitors tasks in order to decide when *Load Shedding* or *Task Re-scheduling* should be triggered. The *QoD Controller* is mainly guided by runtime metrics from the tasks' execution; and by user provided restrictions, i.e. the application queries' *priorities* and *minimum acceptable accuracies*. Decisions from these components are guided by a model that will be detailed in the following sections.

The two components run on the JM (2). The *Task Scheduler* executes for every task scheduling request. While the *QoD Controller* is triggered periodically, possibly sending messages to the TM, either telling them to fail tasks or tune the tasks' load shedders. Note that at a given instant, only one of the JM is the leader, the others are in standby in order to provide high availability. Following that, at a given instant, only the *Task Scheduler* and *QoD Controller* of the leader JM will be executing.

All the TM periodically send runtime metrics to the leader JM (3), such as their CPU usage and the input/output rate of each task instance. These metrics are exposed to the main components, to help them on guiding their decisions.

The Flink stream processing DSL / Programming Model (1) is also extended. This allows the user to define the queries' restrictions. These restrictions are then propagated to the JM, for the *QoD Controller* to take them into account.

As said previously, a load shedding mechanism is also introduced at the applications' runtime level. Thus, allowing them to eventually drop some of the incoming workload. Load shedding has been subject of study in several other works, such as [5] and [23].

3   Stream Economics Model.

In this section, we formalize the concepts and nomenclature that will be used. We use $t(i)$ to refer to the task whose i is instance of; $tm(i)$ as the TM where the task instance i is executing, and $taskManagers$ for all the TM in the system; $queries$ as the set of all query tasks; and $downstream(t)$ / $upstream(t)$ for the downstream / upstream tasks of a task t, that are directly connected to it.

Restrictions. As said, for each query in an application, users are able to specify two restrictions that will be taken into consideration by the system.

Priority - p(t) Each task's priority is defined as $p(t) \in \mathbb{Z}$, computed as described in Eq. 1, where $queries(t)$ corresponds to the set of downstream queries of a task t. The priority is specified by the user for each query and then propagated through their upstream.

$$p(t) = \max_{t' \in queries(t)} p(t') \tag{1}$$

To refer to the set of all tasks' priorities in the system, sorted in descending order, we use $priorities$. Values in this set can be scoped to a specific TM using $priorities(tm)$. We use $ti(tm, p)$ as the set of task instances in a TM tm with priority p; or $ti(tm)$ for all instances regardless of their priority. Additionally, $tm(p)$ is used to represent all the TM that execute task instances with priority p.

Minimum Accuracy - minAc(t). Each query q is also parameterized by the user with the minimum accuracy it accepts, $minAc(q) \in [0\%, 100\%]$. This value corresponds to the minimum percentage of input tuples of the application that must be processed to compute the query output. This is the definition of accuracy that we will follow throughout this paper. Equation 2 shows how this value is propagated throughout the query upstream.

$$minAc(t) = \max_{q \in queries(t)} minAc(q) \tag{2}$$

Load Shedding. Load shedding is performed by using random drops, where each load shedder is parameterized with the probability of keeping an event, named the *non-drop probability* $d(t, t')$, between a producer task t and a consumer task t'.

The percentage of application input events being processed by a specific task t is given by $ac(t)$, which corresponds to our definition of accuracy of the task. To avoid biased results, due to different non-drop probabilities in task instances of the same task, decisions are performed at the task level. Therefore: for two connected instances $i1$ and $i2$ of different tasks $t1$ and $t2$, respectively, $d(i1, i2) = d(t1, t2)$; and $\forall_{i \in instances(t)} ac(i) = ac(t)$, where $instances(t)$ correspond to all instances of a task t.

Additionally, given two tasks $t1$ and $t2$, directly connected to a downstream task $t3$, then $ac(t1) = ac(t2)$ and $ac(t3) \leq ac(t1), ac(t2)$. Essentially, this restriction avoids biased results for tasks that consume data from two or more streams.

Current Accuracy - cAc(t). The current accuracy, $cAc(t) \in [0\%, 100\%]$, is used as a guideline that provides an approximation to the runtime accuracy of a given task t, based on the runtime metrics of the application. Thus, providing a hint on how much overloaded a task is. The system will attempt to maximize $cAc(t)$ at all time.

We define this function as presented in Eq. 3 which is computed using $lAc(t)$, defined in Eq. 4, that represents what we call the local accuracy of a task t.

It's important to note that, according to our definition, the current accuracy of a task is calculated using the minimum current accuracy of its upstream tasks. Meaning that if a task has two upstream branches with different current accuracies, its current accuracy is determined by the minimum, because this is the most that is currently being guaranteed.

$$cAc(t) = \begin{cases} lAc(t), \text{if } upstream(t) = \{\} \\ lAc(t) \times min_{t' \in upstream(t)} cAc(t'), \text{otherwise} \end{cases} \quad (3)$$

$$lAc(t) = \frac{min_{i \in instances(t)} inRate(i)}{\left(\sum_{t' \in upstream(t)} outRate(t', t) \right) / |instances(t)|} \quad (4)$$

Regarding Eq. 4, the $inRate(i)$ represents the input rate of an instance i of a task t; while $outRate(t', t)$ corresponds to the output rate of an upstream task t' to a task t. Therefore, the local accuracy of a task matches the minimum local accuracy of its instances, with the assumption that the output rate of its upstream is fairly distributed over its task instances. Additionally, if the denominator of the Eq. 4 equals zero then, $lAc(t) = 100\%$. This happens because in that case t is consuming all its input, i.e. none.

The objective is therefore to minimize the difference between a task upstream output rate and its input rate — maximize the overall application throughput.

Maximum Achievable Accuracy - maxAc(t). Given the desired accuracy for each downstream query q, represented as $desired(q)$, $maxAc(t)$ returns the maximum accuracy that the upstream task t will have, based on the restrictions imposed by the downstream queries and taking into account that events will be dropped as soon as possible in the DAG. The way this it is computed is described in Eq. 5.

$$maxAc(t) = \max_{q \in queries(t)} desired(q) \tag{5}$$

CPU Load. The decisions of the *QoD Controller* are guided by the CPU usage and accuracy metrics from the applications' runtime. With the accuracy already defined in the previous section, it only remains to define the part of our model that takes into account the CPU runtime metrics.

The expected CPU load for a task t, cpu(t), is computed as described in Eq. 6 where $cpuMetric(i) \in [0\%, 100\%]$ corresponds to the CPU load obtained from the TM metrics, for a task instance i. If a task is using a full CPU virtual core, then $cpu(t) = 100\%$.

Since the local accuracy, defined in the previous section, is restricted by the minimum local accuracy of the task's instances, $cpu(t)$ is also restricted by the CPU load of this same instance. Additionally, we assume that all TM have identical computational capacity. Thus, in a stable system the CPU load should be similar for all instances of the same task.

$$cpu(t) = cpuMetric \left(_{i' \in instances(t)} inRate(i') \right) \tag{6}$$

We also define: $cpu(tm)$ as the CPU usage of the TM, including non-Flink processes; $tCpu(tm) = \sum_{i \in ti(tm)} cpu(i)$; and $nCores(tm)$ as the amount of CPU virtual cores provided by a TM tm.

Minimum Obtained CPU - mObtCpu(i). The minimum CPU amount a task instance i is guaranteed to get, $mObtCpu(i)$, based on the current available CPU, $aCpu(tm)$, of the respective TM, tm. It is computed as in Eq. 7. The available CPU time is evenly distributed over all tasks with the same priority. Note that a task may require less CPU resources than the ones it can get, in order to achieve the accuracy that it requires.

$$mObtCpu(i) = \frac{aCpu(tm(i))}{|ti(tm(i), p(t(i)))|} \tag{7}$$

Required CPU - rCpu(t, ac) The CPU required by a task t in order to have $ac(t) = ac$ is represented as $rCpu(t, ac)$. The function is defined in Eq. 8, and assumes that the CPU load and accuracy are proportional.

$$rCpu(t, ac) = \begin{cases} 0, \text{if } cAc(t) = 0\% \text{ and } ac = 0\% \\ 100, \text{if } cAc(t) = 0\% \text{ and } ac \neq 0\% \\ \min \left(\frac{ac \times cpu(t)}{cAc(t)}, 100 \right), \text{otherwise} \end{cases} \tag{8}$$

In the first condition the required CPU is 0% since no accuracy is required. In the second one we provide our best bet on the required CPU, 100% (a full virtual CPU core).

Additionally, we also define the required CPU to achieve the minimum, $minAc(t)$, and maximum accuracies, $maxAc(t)$. Computed as presented in Eqs. 9 and 10, respectively.

$$minReqCpu(t) = rCpu(t, minAc(t)) \qquad (9)$$

$$maxReqCpu(t) = rCpu(t, maxAc(t)) \qquad (10)$$

Obtained Accuracy - obtAc(t, cpu). Given a task t and a provided CPU load, cpu, $obtAc(t, cpu)$ returns the maximum accuracy the task can provide to its downstream using that CPU amount, as expressed in Eq. 11. Once again, it assumes the CPU load and the accuracy of the task to be proportional.

$$obtAc(t, cpu) = \begin{cases} 0\%, \text{if } cAc(t) = 0\% \text{ and cpu} = 0 \\ 100\%, \text{if } cAc(t) = 0\% \text{ and cpu} \neq 0 \\ cAc(t), \text{if } cpu(t) = 0 \text{ and cpu} = 0 \\ 100\%, \text{if } cpu(t) = 0 \text{ and cpu} \neq 0 \\ \min\left(\frac{cAc(t) \times cpu}{cpu(t)}, 100\%\right), \text{otherwise} \end{cases} \qquad (11)$$

The rationale for the conditions is that: the first and second conditions are aligned with the logic followed in $rCpu(t, ac)$; the third, because if the current and provided accuracies are equal, then the accuracy should remain the same; and the fourth is an optimistic bet on the obtained accuracy.

Slack - slack(tm, p). For a given TM, tm, $slack(tm, p)$ represents the sum of the differences between: the CPU percentage that its tasks with priority p require, in order to achieve the maximum accuracy they can, based on current restrictions imposed by other tasks and while assuming the minimum accuracy is guaranteed; and the available CPU for the task. The way this is done is presented on Eqs. 12 and 13.

$$diffReq(t) = maxReqCpu(t) - minReqCpu(t) \qquad (12)$$

$$slack(tm, p) = \sum_{i \in ti(tm,p)} (diffReq(t(i)) - mObtCpu(t(i))) \qquad (13)$$

4   QoD Controller

The *QoD Controller* periodically executes Algorithm 1, which is defined in several steps. In each iteration, it starts by initializing the available CPU as the total available CPU for each TM to execute Flink tasks; and the desired accuracy for each query as 100%, since it hasn't yet pruned it with Load Shedding (lines 1–6).

Algorithm 1. QoD Controller main cycle.

1: **for all** $tm \in taskManagers$ **do**
2:     $aCpu(tm) \leftarrow 100 \times nCores(tm) - cpu(tm) + tCpu(tm)$
3: **end for**
4: **for all** $q \in queries$ **do**
5:     $desired(q) \leftarrow 100\%$
6: **end for**
7: **for all** $tm \in taskManagers$ **do**
8:     $reqCpu \leftarrow \sum_{i \in ti(tm)} minReqCpu(t(i))$
9:     $rel \leftarrow 0$
10:     **if** $reqCpu > aCpu(tm)$ **then**
11:         $rel \leftarrow killTasks(reqCpu - aCpu(tm), tm)$
12:     **end if**
13:     $aCpu(tm) \leftarrow aCpu(tm) - reqCpu + rel$
14: **end for**
15: **for all** $p \in priorities$ **do**
16:     **for all** $tm \in tm(p)$ by $slack(tm, p)$ DESC **do**
17:         $distributeEvenly(ti(tm, p), aCpu, desired)$
18:     **end for**
19: **end for**
20: Compute $d(t, t')$ based on the queries' desired accuracy
21: Send new $d(t, t')$ to the Task Managers where t is running

---

The algorithm then proceeds to guarantee that each TM has the necessary CPU to run all its task instances regardless of their priorities (lines 7–14). If there's not enough CPU, it releases the necessary CPU by re-scheduling some tasks (lines 10–12). Once each task is guaranteed to have its minimum accuracy, the algorithm distributes the remaining available CPU over the task instances (lines 15–19), this time respecting their priorities. It starts by the TM with highest slack to avoid having to backtrack already made decisions. Finally, the non-drop probabilities for all streams are computed, using the method described in Sect. 5.3, and sent to the TM to adjust the load shedders (lines 20 and 21).

Task Re-scheduling. To select which tasks to re-schedule, given a TM and the amount of CPU to release, we use Algorithm 2. This is done in two steps. The first one aims at determining the maximum priority of the tasks that may have to be re-scheduled to release at least the required CPU load (lines 3–8). It returns a set of candidate tasks to be re-scheduled, and the released CPU if all those tasks are actually re-scheduled.

The second step (lines 9–16) avoids releasing more CPU than necessary, by pruning the candidate tasks set. It starts by the tasks with higher priority and higher required CPU. If by removing the task from the set, it still allows to release at least the amount of CPU that must be released, then, we remove it. Otherwise, the task instance is failed, in order to be re-scheduled to another TM. At this point, the released CPU by re-scheduling a task instance corresponds to the one used to achieve its minimum accuracy.

Also notice that the algorithm prefers to re-schedule tasks with low CPU consumption. The reason we opt for this semantic is because: 1) it reduces resource fragmentation; 2) smaller tasks are easier to re-schedule since they require less

---

Algorithm 2. Selection of tasks to be re-scheduled.

```
 1: function KILLTASKS(cpu, tm)
 2:     rel ← 0, I ← {}
 3:     for all p ∈ priorities(tm) do
 4:         if cpu − rel > 0 then
 5:             I ← I ∪ ti(tm, p)
 6:             rel ← rel + ∑_{i∈ti(tm,p)} minReqCpu(t(i))
 7:         end if
 8:     end for
 9:     for all i ∈ I by p(t) DESC, minReqCpu(t(i)) DESC do
10:         if rel − minReqCpu(t(i)) ≥ cpu then
11:             rel ← rel − minReqCpu(t(i))
12:         else
13:             fail(i)
14:             cpu ← cpu − minReqCpu(t(i))
15:         end if
16:     end for
17:     return release
18: end function
```

Algorithm 3. Fair distribution of CPU.

```
 1: function DISTRIBUTEEVENLY(it, aCpu, desired)
 2:     c ← 0
 3:     T ← it by rCpu(i, maxAc(i)) − minReqCpu(t(i)) INC
 4:     for all i ∈ T do
 5:         maxReq ← maxReqCpu(t(i)) − minReqCpu(t(i))
 6:         cpu ← min (maxReq, (aCpu(tm(i)))/(|it|−c))
 7:         ac ← obtAc(i, cpu) + minAc(i)
 8:         for all q ∈ queries(t(i)) do
 9:             desired(q) ← min (desired(q), ac)
10:         end for
11:         aCpu(tm(i)) ← aCpu(tm(i)) − cpu
12:         c ← c + 1
13:     end for
14: end function
```

---

resources; 3) once re-scheduled, these tasks should take less time to recover and start coping again with their incoming workload.

Resource Management. To distribute the remaining CPU of a TM over the task instances, Algorithm 3 is used. The algorithm receives as input the available CPU load to distribute, $aCpu$; the set of tasks over which it should be distributed, it; and the desired accuracies for all tasks in the system, *desired*. It starts by distributing the CPU load by the tasks with lower required CPU to achieve the accuracy they need, avoiding decision backtracking (line 3) since these tasks may require less CPU to achieve their maximum accuracy than the CPU they can get. If such tasks exist, then the remaining CPU from those tasks is fairly distributed across the remaining task instances. During the traversal the desired accuracy for the queries and the available CPU of the TM are updated (line 9).

Computing the Drop Probabilities. To compute the non-drop probabilities for each stream, based on the desired accuracy for each query, we use Eqs. 14

and 15. The first one propagates the dropping probabilities upstream, allowing to drop events as soon as possible in the DAG, thus avoiding processing tuples that will be dropped in the downstream of the applications. After that, the second equation is used to compute the value of the non-drop probability of each load shedder, $d(t, t')$, given the already provided accuracy and the desired accuracy at the downstream task t', $desired(t')$. Note that $d(t, t')$ is also defined for the first load shedder in the source tasks, as the desired accuracy of its associated source task.

$$desired(t) = \max_{t' \in downstream(t)} desired(t') \tag{14}$$

$$d(t, t') = \begin{cases} desired(t'), & \text{if } t \text{ is an external datasource} \\ \frac{desired(t')}{desired(t)}, & \text{otherwise} \end{cases} \tag{15}$$

5   Evaluation

To test the solution, two applications where developed, whose DAG is presented in Fig. 2, both consuming data from Apache Kafka:

1. **TD:** receives two streams of events with information regarding taxi drives, that are consumed by two CPU intensive tasks, $TDSnk1$ and $TDSnk2$, using a *union* operator. $TDSnk2$ is configured with a parallelism of 2, while the remaining tasks have a parallelism of 1.
2. **KNN:** KNN algorithm implementation with a single task, to test the integration with Apache Kafka.

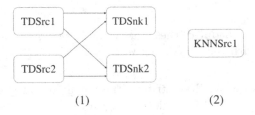

(1)   (2)

Fig. 2. Logical DAG of the Taxi Drives (1) and KNN (2) applications.

We start by running some scenarios to check that the mechanism has the desired features, showing the expected behavior of the system, as well as scenarios where it can reduce resource wastage and improve tasks' performance by detecting resource starvation situations. The second part aims at evaluating the performance impact in the JM, and the *QoD Controller*.

The evaluation environment consists in four machines: one for Apache Kafka and the data injector; one JM; and two TM. Each machine has a dedicated virtual CPU, in a quad-core Intel Core i7, and 3Gb memory each. The *QoD Scheduler* was configured with a 5 s frequency.

Scenario 1: Tasks with Same Priorities. Our first scenario is an execution of the TD application, with $minAc(TDSnk1) = 40\%$ and $minAc(TDSnk2) = 60\%$, where all tasks have equal priority. Figure 3.a) shows the obtained results.

The system starts with a single TM, $TM1$, thus causing all TD's tasks to be scheduled to it. Later (A), the second TM, $TM2$, is added to the system, without any tasks being immediately scheduled to it. As the workload of the application increases to levels where the application can't cope with, the load shedding mechanism is triggered, causing the application accuracy to decrease (A). Every time the workload decreases, the accuracy of the application increases, up to the moment where load shedding is no longer required (B). In (A), the effect of all sinks having the same priority is clear, since load shedding is being applied to both sinks, without any of them reaching their accuracy threshold.

In instants (C) and (D) the *QoD Controller* decides to re-schedule some tasks to the later added TM. In (C) the first instance of the $TDSnk1$ was re-scheduled, while in (D) it was the second instance of the same task. Yielding an optimal task distribution that maximizes both the throughput and accuracy of the application, and reduces resource wastage. Both $TDSnk1$ instances where re-scheduled instead of $TDSnk2$, which happens because their re-scheduling minimized the amount of released CPU while still releasing enough for the remaining tasks in $TM1$ to keep up with their workload.

The effects of the tasks' warmup state in the accuracy are visible every time a task is re-scheduled. All tasks took less than 1 min to exit this state.

During the execution, we observed that the difference between $currAc$ $(TDSrc1)$ and $ac(TDSrc1)$, and between $currAc(TDSrc2)$ and $ac(TDSrc2)$, was on average 2.4% and 1.8%, respectively.

Scenario 2: Tasks with Different Priorities. The second scenario shows an execution of both TD and KNN applications, where their tasks have distinct priorities. This allows to observe how priorities are taken into account by the system. The KNN application was executed with a single instance.

As shown in Fig. 3.b), the scenario starts with both TM available, and the TD application's tasks scheduled among them based on the scheduling policy. The KNN application is added later (A), being scheduled to the TM2, the one with more available resources. Once the KNN application is scheduled, the effect of its warmup state is visible on the other tasks executing in the same TM.

It is also visible that the $TDSnk1$ task has a higher priority than the $KNNSrc1$ task. When the KNN application workload increases (B), its accuracy also drops, while the accuracy of the $TDSnk1$ task remains unchanged. A similar behaviour appears after instant (C), the KNN application's accuracy drops to release resources for the $TDSnk1$.

The $TDSnk1$ task also has a lower priority than the $TDSnk2$. As their workload increases, $TDSnk1$ instances' accuracy drops before load shedding triggers on $TDSnk2$, eventually re-scheduling the first $TDSnk1$ task instance (C) in order to allow $TDSnk2$ to keep up with its workload.

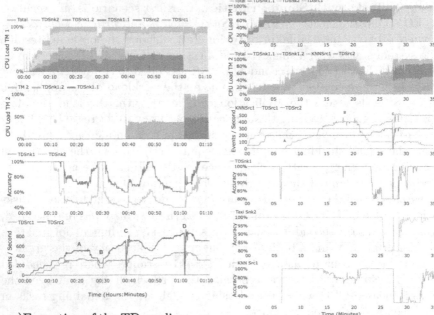

a.)Execution of the TD application where all sinks have the same priority. First two charts show the CPU
load of each TM and their executing
tasks. Third and fourth charts show
the application sinks' accuracy and
the application throughput for each
input Kafka topic, respectively.

b.)TD and KNN applications
execution, having tasks with different
priorities. First two charts show the
CPU load in both TM. Third chart
shows the applications' throughput for
each input Kafka topic. The accuracy
for each sink task is presented in the
remaining charts.

Fig. 3. Task Performance with identical and different priorities.

Once again this scenario shows the ability of our system to adapt task
scheduling based on the runtime requirements of application tasks, increasing
the overall throughput. Flink is incapable of performing this type of adapta-
tion, clearly showing a situation where our system performs better in terms of
resource efficiency.

Performance Assessment. In terms of performance impact of our mechanism,
we analyzed the impact on the JM' resource usage. We focused on understanding
if our mechanism scales with the amount of tasks being executed in the system.
The results presented in both Figs. 4.a) and 4.b) show this assessment. The first
shows how the CPU load of the JM increases as the amount of tasks being executed increases. The second shows how the execution time of the *QoD Controller*
monitoring cycle increases with the amount of executing tasks.

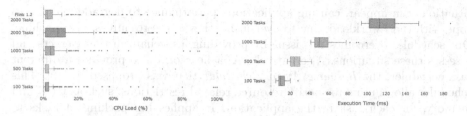

a.)CPU Load of the JM for different amounts of executing tasks, with two TM, and comparison with Flink.

b.)Execution time of the *QoD Controller*, given a fixed amount of executing tasks and using two TM.

Fig. 4. CPU Load of the JM and Execution time of the QoD Controller.

The results show that even with 2000 executing tasks, the JM's CPU load is below 15% in the third quartile and that the execution time of the *QoD Controller* is below 115 ms in the second quartile. Therefore, our mechanism can clearly scale to environments running thousands of tasks in parallel. When compared with Flink, in first row in Fig. 4.a), our solution is more CPU intensive.

6   Related Work

In Apache Flink, each TM provides a set of *slots* [2, 7] that can be used to execute tasks. There is no CPU isolation between slots. Slots simply limit the amount of tasks that can be executed in the TM. Flink scheduling strategy assigns tasks to all slots in a TM, only then moves to the next one. This approach only succeeds if the characteristics of the tasks that will be deployed to the cluster are well known. If tasks are expected to consume few resources, then the TM should provide a higher amount of slots, avoiding underutilization of the available resources. If they are expected to consume lots of resources, then slots should be coarse grained, since its expected for these tasks to consume all the available resources, thus avoiding resource starvation. In Flink, tasks of the same application can share slots with *Slot Sharing*. Thus, allowing to group fine grained tasks and run them in a coarse grained slot, reducing the probability of underutilization. Nonetheless, it is up to the user, that defines the application, to enable or disable slot sharing.

Apache Spark [3] also follows a resource allocation based model, where the resource reservation is defined individually for each application, thus being a more flexible model than the one used by Apache Flink. Nonetheless it can still suffer from resource overallocation, and provides no way to define how to arbitrate over-committed resources among applications in order to maintain latencies and accuracy goals.

Apache Storm's [4] default scheduling strategy consists in a naive round robin distribution of tasks on the available machines. Though this strategy is simple and doesn't require any specific input from the user, resource starvation situations can appear, causing applications performance to degrade and fail to cope with their workload, due to over-utilization of the resources in a machine. Our scheduler overcomes this issue by providing a mechanism that detects and assesses these situations. Alternatively, Apache Storm also provides a different task scheduler, the *Resource Aware Scheduler* that was proposed in [18]. This scheduler allows users to specify resource related restrictions, such as CPU and memory, for each task in the application. It applies bin packing of tasks to the available machines while taking into consideration their needs. With this approach tasks are guaranteed to get the resources they need, but it can suffer from resource underutilization.

More similar to our solution, Apache Mesos *Dynamic Oversubscription* model [1], allows the execution of best-effort tasks in reserved but unused resources. In this model, cluster resources are monitored to detect oversubscribed resources, and to make sure that the revocable tasks don't interfere with the regular tasks. If they do, these revocable tasks can be killed or throttled in order to correct the QoS. Similar techniques have been proposed in other systems such as [14]. Both these solutions can't take advantage of load shedding, allowing application to provide fresh results even in peak load situations, as they are not specific for stream processing use cases. Nonetheless, they highlight the necessity of monitoring applications' QoS when using task overallocation as a solution to avoid resource wastage, to guarantee that applications' QoS is respected. Eventual corrections to the QoS are performed by a compensation mechanism. This same pattern can be found in [20].

On a more academic context of big data analytics [16], several works can be found regarding resource efficiency in large scale data processing clusters, but none of them actually leverages load shedding as a tool to guarantee the applications' QoS in overallocation situations, as we review some next. In [22] a model is proposed to estimate applications' resource allocation needs based on a priori knowledge of the applications, also used to drive resource mapping. Other solutions, such as the ones introduced in [11], focus on estimating the actual available resources, avoiding resource wastage scenarios; and in the work in [21] with additional employ of game theory to drive container allocation that host streaming applications. Resource management can also take advantage of hidden Markov models to forecast frequent patterns and approximate computation, albeit with 72% average accuracy [13].

Alternative approaches include determining ideal configurations for applications, such as application parallelism [12], and recommend them to the users, avoiding resource over-estimation, or with automatic parameter tuning [15]; determine load shedding factors with machine learning that ensure a specific error bound in continuous Map-Reduce workflows [9]; apply load shedding to iterative graph processing [8]; and even developing novel intermediate data structures to accelerate big-data workloads such as multi-label classification [10].

As a whole, current resource management solutions for distributed stream processing systems lack the ability to dynamically adapt tasks' scheduling based on their runtime metrics, data accuracy and resource efficiency. This happens to be a key factor to improve overall resource efficiency in data processing clusters, more so when resources are being paid for in cloud computing deployments.

7   Conclusions

We proposed a novel task scheduling strategy for stream processing systems such as Apache Flink. Our strategy specifically targets the problem of resource under-utilization that current solutions fail to overcome. Benchmarks of our mechanism show promising results as they show that our strategy is able to adapt tasks' assignments to the available machines, converging towards a task distribution that not only reduces resource wastage, but also improves the applications' throughput in situations of resource starvation.

The developed load shedding mechanism also proved to be valuable, as it enables applications to keep up with their incoming workload without having to immediately re-schedule them for them to cope with it. At the same time, the load shedding mechanism is able to take into account different requirements from each sink in an application, avoiding processing events that will be dropped later in the application's downstream. Thus, being a good additional contribution from this paper.

We consider that future work should focus on overcoming identified restrictions, exploring alternative semantics for the different components of the proposed mechanism, or even allowing these different semantics to be customizable. For instance, allowing users to provide their own definition of accuracy and of current accuracy for each application; or even enable applications to use different load shedding strategies, e.g. semantic load shedding.

Acknowledgements. This work was supported by national funds through FCT, Fundação para a Ciência e a Tecnologia, under project UIDB/50021/2020 (DOI:10.54499/UIDB/50021/2020). This work was supported by: "DL 60/2018, de 3–08 - Aquisição necessária para a atividade de I&D do INESC-ID, no âmbito do projeto SmartRetail (C6632206063-00466847)". This work was supported by the CloudStars project, funded from the European Union's Horizon research and innovation program under grant agreement number 101086248.

References

1. Apache Mesos. Mesos oversubscription. http://mesos.apache.org/documentation/latest/oversubscription/
2. Apache Software Foundation. Apache flink. http://flink.apache.org
3. Apache Software Foundation. Apache spark. http://spark.apache.org
4. Apache Software Foundation. Apache storm. http://storm.apache.org
5. Babcock, B., Datar, M., Motwani, R.: Load shedding for aggregation queries over data streams. In: Proceedings of the 20th International Conference on Data Engineering. ICDE '04, pp. 350–361, Washington, DC, USA, IEEE Computer Society (2004)

6. Baset, S.A., Wang, L., Tang, C.: Towards an understanding of oversubscription in cloud. In: Hot-ICE (2012)
7. Carbone, P., Katsifodimos, A., Ewen, S., Markl, V., Haridi, S., Tzoumas, K.: Apache flink: stream and batch processing in a single engine. Data Eng. **38**(4) (2015)
8. Coimbra, M.E., Esteves, S., Francisco, A.P., Veiga, L.: Veilgraph: incremental graph stream processing. J. Big Data **9**(1), 23 (2022)
9. Esteves, S., Galhardas, H., Veiga, L.: Adaptive execution of continuous and data-intensive workflows with machine learning. In: Proceedings of the 19th International Middleware Conference. Middleware '18, pp. 239–252, New York, NY, USA, Association for Computing Machinery (2018)
10. Gonzalez-Lopez, J., Ventura, S., Cano, A.: Distributed nearest neighbor classification for large-scale multi-label data on spark. Futur. Gener. Comput. Syst. **87**, 66–82 (2018)
11. Ha, S.H., Brown, P., Michiardi, P.: Resource management for parallel processing frameworks with load awareness at worker side. In: Big Data (BigData Congress), 2017 IEEE International Congress on, pp. 161–168. IEEE (2017)
12. Á. B. Hernández, M. S. Perez, S. Gupta, V. Muntés-Mulero.: Using machine learning to optimize parallelism in big data applications. Future Gener. Comput. Syst. (2017)
13. Liu, C.M., Liao, K.T.: Efficiently predicting frequent patterns over uncertain data streams. Procedia Comput. Sci. **160**, 15–22. The 10th International Conference on Emerging Ubiquitous Systems and Pervasive Networks (EUSPN-2019) / The 9th International Conference on Current and Future Trends of Information and Communication Technologies in Healthcare (ICTH-2019) / Affiliated Workshops (2019)
14. Lo, D., Cheng, L., Govindaraju, R., Ranganathan, P., Kozyrakis, C.: Heracles: improving resource efficiency at scale. In: ACM SIGARCH Computer Architecture News. vol. 43, pp. 450–462. ACM (2015)
15. Lu, J., Chen, Y., Herodotou, H., Babu, S.: Speedup your analytics: automatic parameter tuning for databases and big data systems. Proc. VLDB Endow. **12**(12), 1970–1973 (2019)
16. Mohamed, A., Najafabadi, M.K., Wah, Y.B., Zaman, E.A.K., Maskat, R.: The state of the art and taxonomy of big data analytics: view from new big data framework. Artif. Intell. Rev. **53**(2), 989–1037 (2020)
17. Moreno, I.S., Xu, J.: Customer-aware resource overallocation to improve energy efficiency in realtime cloud computing data centers. In: Service-Oriented Computing and Applications (SOCA), 2011 IEEE International Conference on, pp. 1–8. IEEE (2011)
18. Peng, B., Hosseini, M., Hong, Z., Farivar, R., Campbell, R.: R-Storm: resource-aware scheduling in storm. In: Proceedings of the 16th Annual Middleware Conference. Middleware '15, pp. 149–161, New York, NY, USA, ACM (2015)
19. Reiss, C., Tumanov, A., Ganger, G.R., Katz, R.H., Kozuch, M.A.: Heterogeneity and dynamicity of clouds at scale: Google trace analysis. In: Proceedings of the Third ACM Symposium on Cloud Computing, pp. 7. ACM (2012)
20. Runsewe, O., Samaan, N.: loud resource scaling for big data streaming applications using a layered multi-dimensional hidden markov model. In: Cluster, Cloud and Grid Computing (CCGRID), 2017 17th IEEE/ACM International Symposium on, pp. 848–857. IEEE (2017)

21. Runsewe, O., Samaan, N.: Cram: a container resource allocation mechanism for big data streaming applications. In: 2019 19th IEEE/ACM International Symposium on Cluster, Cloud and Grid Computing (CCGRID), pp. 312–320, Los Alamitos, CA, USA, IEEE Computer Society (2019)

22. Shukla, A., Simmhan, Y.L.: Model-driven scheduling for distributed stream processing systems. CoRR. abs/1702.01785 (2017)

23. Tatbul, N., U. Çetintemel, Zdonik, S., Cherniack, M., Stonebraker, M.: Load shedding in a data stream manager. In: Proceedings of the 29th International Conference on Very Large Data Bases-vol. 29, pp. 309–320. VLDB Endowment (2003)

Synql: A CRDT-Based Approach for Replicated Relational Databases with Integrity Constraints

Claudia-Lavinia Ignat[✉], Victorien Elvinger, and Habibatou Ba

Inria, Université de Lorraine, CNRS, LORIA, 54500 Nancy, France
claudia.ignat@inria.fr

Abstract. Many offline-first applications use an embedded relational database, such as SQLite, to manage their data. The replication of the database eases the addition of collaborative features to its applications. Most of the approaches for replicating a relational database require coordination at some extent. A few approaches propose a coordination-less replication to allow offline work. These approaches are limited in two ways: (i) They do not respect *Strong Eventual Consistency* that states that two replicas converge as soon as they integrate the same set of modifications; (ii) They fail to preserve the combined effect of operations' intent in complex scenarios. We propose Synql, an approach based on Conflict-free Replicated Data Types (CRDTs) that addresses these two limitations. Synql relies on a replicated state defined by the composition of CRDT primitives. The state of the database is computed over the replicated state. The user modifications are compensated so that the computed state corresponds to what the users saw and changed.

1 Introduction

The pandemic and the generalisation of remote working led to a massive adoption of applications that dematerialize workspaces. These applications rely heavily on collaborative features. Adding collaborative features to existing applications is hard. Local-first software approach proved its simplicity and efficiency in adding collaboration to existing applications by replicating the application data without knowing the application internals [13].

Many applications use embedded relational databases, such as SQLite, to manage their data. In order to ensure a high availability and low latency, databases are commonly replicated [8,9]. As stated by the CAP theorem [7,10,11] high availability and data consistency is difficult to achieve in distributed systems in the presence of network partitions. Most database systems such as SQL, NewSQL and some NoSQL (e.g. graph databases such as Neo4j) aim to achieve the ACID properties (Atomicity, Consistency, Isolation, Durability) and to maintain a strong consistency by means of serialisability and its many implementations including lock-based and pre-scheduling mechanisms

R. Martins and M. Selimi (Eds.): DAIS 2024, LNCS 14677, pp. 18–35, 2024.
https://doi.org/10.1007/978-3-031-62638-8_2

[19,21,22]. These mechanisms for ensuring strong consistency require coordination which limits data availability and system scalability and increases latency.

Those NoSQL database systems that want to ensure a high data availability relax consistency and they conform to BASE (Basically Available, Soft State, Eventually Consistent) rather than ACID transaction model. They usually implement lazy replication which may result in a situation where reads on replicas might be inconsistent for a short period of time. Voldemort [20] and Cassandra [15] use quorums for achieving consistency which require coordination.

Several applications built upon databases used a weak consistency in order to avoid a costly coordination [3,16]. However, these application invariants might get violated due to concurrent executions of the operations [2]. These applications still use coordination to enforce some integrity constraints. They are therefore impractical for applications that support offline work.

In [24], authors propose Conflict-free Replicated Relations (CRR) where they adapt the Local-First Software [13] for replicating relational databases. This allows the addition of collaborative features to offline-first applications that embed SQLite for handling their data. CRR approach enables concurrent insertions, updates, and deletions without coordination. It presents also a strategy for maintaining the most commonly used integrity constraints: uniqueness integrity and referential integrity. However, it fails to preserve the combined effect of operations' intent in several scenarios. In a collaborative environment, the combined effect of operations' intent represents the ideal merger of individual operations performed on the different replicas. It combines the highest possible number of operations with respect to their original impact on their specific replica state. Moreover, it does not respect *Strong Eventual Consistency (SEC)* [18] – a property that ensures convergence as soon as every replica has integrated the same modifications without further coordination.

We propose a novel solution which combines CRDT primitives with specific merging semantics and compensation mechanisms to ensure *SEC* and preserve the combined effect of operations' intent.

This paper presents the following contributions:

- A scenario-based study of the state of the art which highlights its limitations.
- A definition of the essential requirements necessary for a solution to address these limitations.
- A novel Synql approach based on CRDTs to ensure *SEC* and preserve the combined effect of operations' intent for integrity maintenance in replicated databases.
- A compensation technique to restore deleted tuples when required.

This paper is structured as follows. Firstly, we explore the preservation of integrity constraints in face of concurrency. Next, we introduce Synql, our CRDT-based approach for replication and integrity maintenance. Then, we study and evaluate the related work before concluding the paper in the following section.

2   Integrity Constraints Maintenance

Integrity constraints in a database are rules used to ensure the accuracy and consistency of data in a relational database. These constraints enforce certain conditions that the data in the database must comply with. While there are several types of integrity constraints, in this paper we address uniqueness and referential integrities.

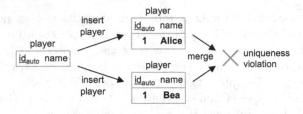

Fig. 1. Uniqueness violation

2.1   Uniqueness Integrity

In a relational database, a unique key is a set of attributes of a relation that uniquely identifies every tuple of the relation. The primary key of a relation is one of its unique keys. Uniqueness integrity ensures that no two tuples in the relation have the same unique key value.

In a replicated context, tuples can be concurrently inserted and updated. This can lead to uniqueness violation during synchronization. In Fig. 1, Alice (A) and Bea (B) concurrently insert a tuple in the relation *player*. They pick the same primary key. The synchronization results in a uniqueness violation.

Some replicated databases such as Invariant Preserving Applications (IPA) [5] only support globally unique identifiers. Others such as AntidoteSQL (AQL) [17] occasionally fall back on coordination when the user wants to achieve strict consistency. AQL relies on the use of specific concurrency semantics to ensure uniqueness integrity.

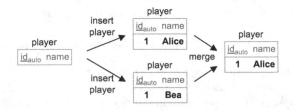

Fig. 2. Maintenance of uniqueness integrity in CRR [24].

During synchronization, CRR [24] applies every modification individually in order to catch integrity violations. Upon a uniqueness violation, the conflict resolver undoes the newest modification that caused the violation. In Fig. 2, we assume that the timestamp of the insertion of Alice is lower than the timestamp of the insertion of Bea. The synchronization preserves the insertion of Alice and undoes the insertion of Bea. This strategy makes the result of a merge sensitive to the order in which the operations are integrated. While CRR maintains uniqueness integrity, it fails to preserve the combined effect of operations' intent (the insertion of Bea is not included in the final state).

Existing databases widely use automatically incremented primary keys as a generic way to identify a tuple. The specific value of these primary keys is generally not relevant. Based on this observation, we handle automatically incremented primary keys differently from other unique keys. We treat them as local identifiers that are not replicated and for which the convergence does not need to be ensured. Distinct replicas can assign distinct keys to a same tuple. In the Fig. 3, the synchronization preserves the two insertions. The tuple inserted by Alice is identified by 1 on the replica A, and it is identified by 2 on the replica B. Conversely, the tuple inserted by Bea is identified by 1 on the replica B, and it is identified by 2 on the replica A.

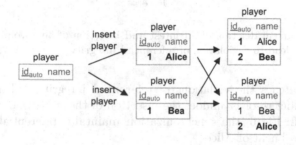

Fig. 3. Proposal for uniqueness integrity of automatically incremented primary keys.

Fig. 4. Example of foreign keys.

2.2 Referential Integrity

In a relational database, a foreign key is a set of attributes in a relation that references the primary key of another relation. In Fig. 4, the foreign key of the relation *game* consists of the attribute *contest* and references the primary key of the relation *contest*. The relation *enrolled* has two foreign keys: one that references the primary key of the relation *player* and another one that references the primary key of the relation *contest*. Referential integrity ensures the existence of the tuples referenced by any tuple. Relational databases allow to customize the behavior of the deletion of a tuple when another tuple references it. The deletion can be aborted or propagated to the referencing tuple.

In a replicated context, the deletion of a tuple and its referencing can happen in concurrence. In Fig. 5, Alice enrolls herself in the contest *C1*, while Bea concurrently deletes *C1*. The synchronization breaks referential integrity.

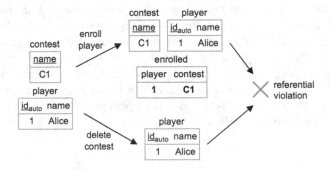

Fig. 5. The concurrent deletion of a contest and insertion of an enrolment that references the contest lead to a violation of referential integrity.

CRR [24] catches the violations of referential integrity. When a violation occurs, the conflict resolver undoes the insertion of the tuple that references the deleted tuple. In Fig. 6, the synchronization maintains referential integrity by undoing the enrolment of Alice.

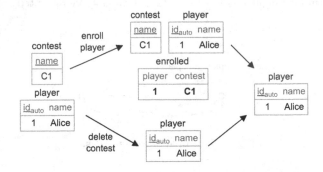

Fig. 6. Maintenance of referential integrity in CRR [24].

This CRR strategy does not support alternative merge semantic in which the insertion of an enrolment wins over the deletion of the referenced contest.

It requires that each operation be applied individually to catch any integrity violation. This limits the possibilities for implementation of state-based [18] or delta-based CRDTs [1]. Moreover, some databases, such as SQLite, do not verify referential integrity in their default configuration. In this case, the synchronization results in a dangling reference as illustrated in Fig. 7.

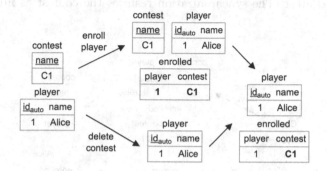

Fig. 7. Dangling reference in SQLite.

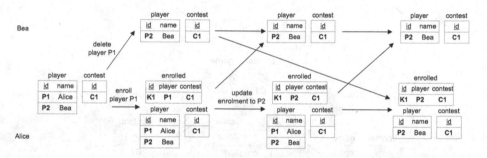

Fig. 8. Divergence of final states in CRR [24].

Moreover, in several scenarios where the same set of operations is executed in different order by the different users, CRR might end up with divergent states. In the scenario in Fig. 8, Alice and Bea start working from the same state of the database consisting of the relation *player* containing *P1* and *P2* and of the relation *contest* containing *C1*. Alice creates an enrolment *E1(K1,P1,C1)*, where the primary key of the *enrolled* relation is an automatically incremented identifier, while Bea removes *P1*. Afterwards, Alice sends her changes to Bea and Bea sends her changes to Alice. When Bea receives the enrolment of player *P1*, the enrolment is deleted as there is an integrity constraint violation as *P1* was deleted. Afterwards, Alice updates the enrolment *E1* to *E1(K1,P2,C1)* and sends her changes to Bea. When Bea receives the update enrolment of Alice, the operation is not executed as *E1* does not exist on the Bea's site. Finally, when Alice receives the deletion of Bea, she executes it. We can notice that, even though Alice and Bea received the same operations, their states diverge. Therefore, CRR does not satisfy SEC.

IPA [5] and AQL [17] propose another approach to maintain referential integrity. The enrolment of Alice embeds a *compensation* that ensures the existence of the contest. The synchronization restores the contest as illustrated in Fig. 9.

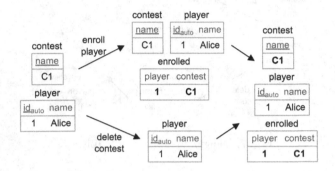

Fig. 9. Maintenance of referential integrity in IPA [5] and AQL [17].

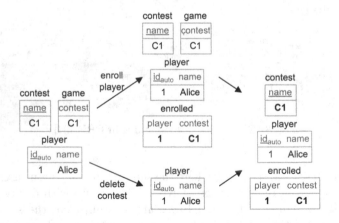

Fig. 10. Limits of compensated operations in IPA [5].

This approach of IPA and AQL preserves referential integrity, but does not preserve the combined effect of operations' intent in other scenarios. In IPA and AQL, respectively Fig. 10 and Fig. 11, a *game* references the contest *C*1. The deletion of *C*1 leads to the deletion of the game (we assume propagated deletions). The synchronization restores the contest $C1$, but does not restore the *game*. This breaks operation intent as the deletion of the contest resulted in the deletion of the game and not the contest. In IPA (Fig. 10), the deleted tuples are directly removed from the computed state, while in AQL (Fig. 11), the deletion is based on visibility flags (I for inserted or updated tuples, T for referenced tuples and D for deleted tuples added to the visibility column "$\#st$").

To preserve the combined effect of operations' intent, we could extend this approach in order to embed the insertion of the game in the enrolment action. However, if a game is concurrently inserted, then we cannot embed its insertion in the enrolment. The proposal of IPA and AQL also allows to choose the alternative merge semantic where the concurrent deletions of a contest and its references lead to the deletion of all referencing enrolments. To do this, the compensation deletes all referencing tuples.

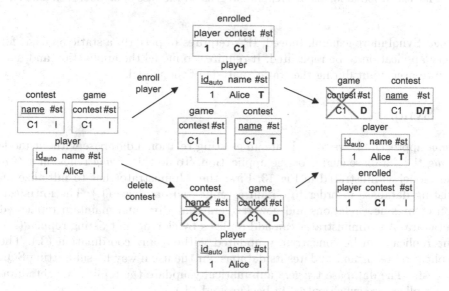

Fig. 11. Limits of compensated operations in AQL [17].

Our proposal takes a different path. Instead of just restoring the contest, it also preserves the game that references the contest as illustrated in Fig. 12. We also leverage existing annotations of the database schema to determine which merge semantic to adopt. If the deletion of a tuple is propagated to its referencing tuple (e.g. DELETE CASCADE in SQLite), then we adopt a *remove-win* semantic. Upon the deletion of a tuple, all referencing tuples, including concurrently inserted tuples, are then deleted. If the deletion is aborted (e.g. DELETE RESTRICT in SQLite), then we adopt an *add-win* semantic. The deleted tuple is restored if a referencing tuple was concurrently inserted.

IPA [5] tries to preserve the application invariants at a high level. Synql preserves low-level invariants (referential integrity and uniqueness integrity). This

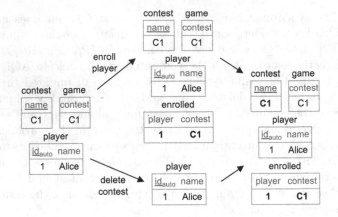

Fig. 12. Proposal for the referential integrity in the case of an abort semantic.

makes Synql more general. Indeed, IPA requires to perform a static analysis for every application to be replicated. It requires to model the application and may require user input during the static analysis of the model.

3   Synql

Synql approach allows to replicate an existing relational database without modifying the database engine or the application. To do this, *Synql* relies on a *Git*-like model as illustrated in Fig. 13. First the administrator has to initialize an existing database in order to obtain a replicated database (1.). The initialization creates new relations and new triggers that store and maintain replicated metadata. An administrator can add replicas by cloning an existing replica (2.). The replicas can be concurrently updated without any coordination (3.). The application reads and updates its database in the usual way by submitting SQL requests. The database triggers automatically update the replicated metadata. The replicas are synchronized in background (4.).

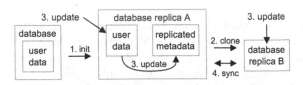

Fig. 13. Architecture of *Synql*.

The basis of the replication system relies on the identification of every inserted tuple with a globally unique identifier consisting of a monotonically increasing timestamp [14] and a unique replica identifier. This is closely related to the concept of *dot* [1] with an important difference: the main component of the identifier is the timestamp instead of the replica identifier. This allows to use its identifiers as timestamps. Thus, we name them *labeled timestamps*. Labeled timestamps are ordered lexicographically. This induces a total order between them. For example, $1_A < 1_B < 2_A < \ldots$ where A, B are replica identifiers and $1, 2$ are timestamps. $\mathbb{N}_{\mathbb{I}}$ denotes the set of labeled timestamps with $\mathbb{I}$ the set of replica identifiers.

Similar to CRR [24], we use Last-Writer-Win (LWW) Registers [12] for replicating tuple attributes. LWW Registers can be created, updated and deleted using the LWW rule to arbitrate between concurrent changes without coordination. LWW ensures a total order of operations, at the cost of losing concurrent updates. An LWW Register is a Conflict-free Replicated Data Type (*CRDT*) that ensures Strong Eventual Consistency [18] – a property that ensures convergence as soon as every replica has integrated the same modifications. As illustrated in Fig. 14, it associates a timestamp to a value (Equation 1). A read returns the value without its timestamp (Equation 2). A write associates to a value a new timestamp (Equation 3). Upon merging, it keeps the value with the most recent timestamp (Equation 4).

$$\text{LWWReg} \stackrel{\text{def}}{=} \text{Value} \times \mathbb{N}_{\mathbb{I}} \tag{1}$$

$$\text{rd}(\langle v, t \rangle) \stackrel{\text{def}}{=} v \tag{2}$$

$$\text{wr}_t(v) \stackrel{\text{def}}{=} \langle v, t \rangle \tag{3}$$

$$\langle v, t \rangle \sqcup \langle v', t' \rangle \stackrel{\text{def}}{=} \langle v, t \rangle \text{ if } t > t' \text{ else } \langle v', t' \rangle \tag{4}$$

Fig. 14. Last-Writer-Win Register [12]

In contrast to CRR [24], *Synql* replicates a foreign key as a single attribute that stores the identifier of the referenced tuple. Also, *Synql* does not replicate auto-incremented attributes. It uses a local mapping to find the local value of an auto-incremented attribute of a tuple from the identifier of the tuple. To avoid any ambiguity, we use the term *field* to denote an attribute of a replicated tuple. For a relation $r \in \text{Rel}$, we denote by $\text{Fields}(r)$ the set of fields of r.

We use the concept of *causal length* [23] to support undoing and redoing insertions. We represent a deletion as an undone insertion. We formalize the concept of *causal length* through a new *CRDT*: the *Causal-Length Flag* (*CLFlag*). The Fig. 15 presents its implementation. The flag consists of a natural number (Equation 5). If the number is odd, then the flag is enabled (Equation 6). The state of the flag is toggled by incrementing by 1 its state (Equation 7 and Equation 8). Upon merging, the maximum number wins (Equation 9).

Our replication model relies on the composition of *delta-based CRDT* primitives [6]. A delta-based CRDT is a variant of CRDTs that optimizes data synchronization by transferring only the recent changes, or *deltas*, rather than the

$$\text{CLFlag} \stackrel{\text{def}}{=} \mathbb{N}_0 \tag{5}$$

$$\text{enabled}(n) \stackrel{\text{def}}{=} \text{odd}(n) \tag{6}$$

$$\text{enable}(n) \stackrel{\text{def}}{=} n \text{ if enabled}(n) \text{ else } n+1 \tag{7}$$

$$\text{disable}(n) \stackrel{\text{def}}{=} n+1 \text{ if enabled}(n) \text{ else } n \tag{8}$$

$$n \sqcup n' \stackrel{\text{def}}{=} max(n,n') \tag{9}$$

Fig. 15. Causal-Length Flag CRDT

$$\langle a,b \rangle \sqcup \langle a',b' \rangle \stackrel{\text{def}}{=} \langle a \sqcup a', b \sqcup b' \rangle \text{ where } \langle a,b \rangle, \langle a',b' \rangle \in A \times B \tag{10}$$

$$m \sqcup m' \stackrel{\text{def}}{=} \{k \mapsto m_\perp(k) \sqcup m'_\perp(k) \mid k \in \text{dom}(m) \cup \text{dom}(m')\} \text{ where } m, m' \in K \hookrightarrow V \tag{11}$$

Fig. 16. CRDT primitives and their merge semantic

entire state or all updates since the last synchronization. In the Fig. 16, we summarize the merge semantic of the primitives we are interested in. The merge of a pair is the point-wise merge of its components (Equation 10). The merge of two maps (partial functions) is the point-wise merge of the values that share the same key (Equation 11). Note that in the merge, each map is extended to a total function that returns the bottom element $\perp$ when the key is not part of the domain of the map, i.e. $m_\perp = m \cup \{k \mapsto \perp \mid \notin \text{dom}(m)\}$.

Figure 17 summarizes our replicated state (Equation 12) and associated δ-mutators. Every replicated tuple is a set of Last-Writer-Win Registers [12] indexed by the fields of a given relation r. Every replicated relation consists of a map that associates to a replicated tuple its identifier, i.e. creation labeled timestamp, and a Causal-Length Flag. When the flag is set, the tuple is marked as deleted. Finally, a replicated database is a set of replicated relations indexed by the relations.

$$\text{RDb} \stackrel{\text{def}}{=} \{r \in Rel\} \hookrightarrow \mathbb{N}_\mathbb{I} \hookrightarrow (\text{Fields}(r) \hookrightarrow \text{LWWReg}) \times \text{CLFlag} \tag{12}$$

$$\text{read}(\{r \mapsto t \mapsto \langle \{f \mapsto reg\}, \text{delFlag} \rangle\}) \stackrel{\text{def}}{=} \{r \mapsto t \mapsto \langle \{f \mapsto \text{rd}(reg)\}, \text{enabled}(\text{delFlag}) \rangle\} \tag{13}$$

$$\text{ins}_t^\delta(\text{db}, r, \{f \mapsto v\}) \stackrel{\text{def}}{=} r \mapsto t \mapsto \langle \{f \mapsto \text{wr}_t(v)\}, \perp \rangle \tag{14}$$

$$\text{del}_t^\delta(\text{db}, r, t') \stackrel{\text{def}}{=} r \mapsto t' \mapsto \langle \perp, \text{enable}(\text{delFlag}) \rangle \text{ where } \langle \_, \text{delFlag} \rangle = \text{db}(r)(t') \tag{15}$$

$$\text{update}_t^\delta(\text{db}, r, t', f, v) \stackrel{\text{def}}{=} r \mapsto t' \mapsto \langle f \mapsto \text{wr}_t(v), \perp \rangle \tag{16}$$

Fig. 17. Replicated State

δ-mutators [1] return the minimal state that encodes the change to propagate and merge. The current labelled timestamp denoted by t is an implicit parameter of the presented mutators. The read (Equation 13) evaluates the registers and the flags. The ins δ-mutator (Equation 14) returns a state that includes a newly inserted tuple of a relation r identified by its creation timestamp t [12]. The del δ-mutator (Equation 15) returns a state that turns on the associated flag (delFlag) of the tuple identified by t' in the relation r. The update δ-mutator (Equation 16) returns a state that updates to v the field f of the tuple identified by t' in the relation r.

Thanks to the composition of $CRDT$ primitives, we obtain a new $CRDT$. However, this $CRDT$ does not guarantee integrity constraints. Indeed, several tuples may share the same unique key and a tuple can reference a deleted tuple. Several approaches, such as CRR [24], change the merge operation in order to ensure integrity constraints. The merge depends on the current state of the replica. This makes their approach Eventual Consistent, but not Strong Eventual Consistent.

Instead of modifying the merge operation, we propose to (deterministically) compute a state without integrity violations from the replicated state. This has the advantage to ensure both integrity constraints and Strong Eventual Consistency. To obtain the computed state, we clone the replicated state and apply successive removals and additions:

1. Remove all replicated tuples marked as deleted.
2. Add replicated tuples transitively referenced by a tuple that is not marked as deleted and has an abort semantic upon the deletion of the referenced tuple.
3. For all set of replicated tuples that have at least one conflicting unique key, keep the oldest (according to their identifiers) one and remove others.
4. Remove all replicated tuples that transitively reference at least one replicated tuple not present in the computed state.

To illustrate the merge of two replicated databases, we revisit the example of the Fig. 12 which represents the user data where Alice enrolled a player and Bea deleted a contest. We identify the replica of Alice as A and the one of Bea as B. The Fig. 18 represents a simplified view of the replicated state. It does not include the timestamps of the registers and depicts a causal length flag only when it is not equal to its initial state 0. Note that every tuple is associated to its identifier _id, e.g. the contest $C1$ is identified by 1_A. Moreover, references use tuple identifiers. For instance, the game identified by 2_A references the contest identified by 1_A. Upon the deletion of the contest 1_A, the replica B marks the contest as deleted by enabling its causal-length flag. The state of the flag is thus 1. Although the contest's deletion is propagated to the game that references it, *Synql* does not mark the game as deleted yet. Its deletion is effective in the computed state (step 4). We talk more about this choice in the following paragraphs. Replica A concurrently enrolls Alice in the contest while replica B deletes the contest. Upon synchronization, the new state of user data is computed from the replicated state. The computed state removes replicated tuples marked as deleted (step 1). Here, only the contest is marked as deleted. We assume that the enrolment has an abort semantic. At step 2, as contest is referencing a non-deleted tuple which has an abort semantic, it is added back in the merged state. The steps 3 and 4 do not change the computed state. In fact, for step 4, as contest is restored at step 2, its deletion is finally not propagated to the game. We end with a computed state in which the deletion of the contest is undone.

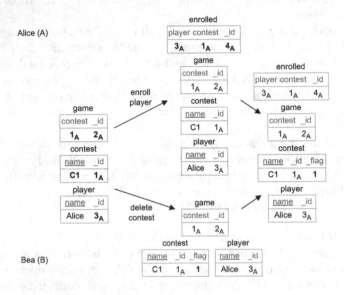

Fig. 18. Example of replicated state merging.

The computation of the database state from the replicated state may lead to surprising effects when local modifications are performed. In the Fig. 18, if a replica deletes the enrolment after the merging, then the contest and the game are also deleted in the computed state. This is due to the fact that the contest is still marked as deleted despite its restoration in the previous computed state. This violates operation intent. To address this issue, local modifications must be compensated. In the previous example, as the deletion of the enrolment will impact the referenced contest, the insertion of the contest has to be redone when performing the deletion. This is achieved by incrementing the delete flag of the referenced tuple by one as illustrated in Fig. 19.

A compensation is applied in two cases: (i) the deletion or the update of a foreign key that uses an abort semantic, (ii) the insertion of a tuple which references another tuple marked as deleted but present in the database state. In the first case, the compensation marks all tuples that are referenced by the reference as non-deleted, if those tuples are also referenced by a tuple not marked as deleted. For example, if the game is previously deleted at one replica (Fig. 20), then the compensation would behave as illustrated in Fig. 21. As the game is already marked as deleted, the deletion of the enrolment would not lead to a constraint violation (since both contest and game are marked as deleted).

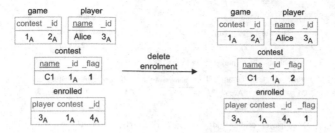

Fig. 19. Example of compensated deletion

Moreover, if the deletion of the enrolment led to the compensation of both the contest and the game, then that would break the initial operation intent and counteract the effect of the game deletion at replica A.

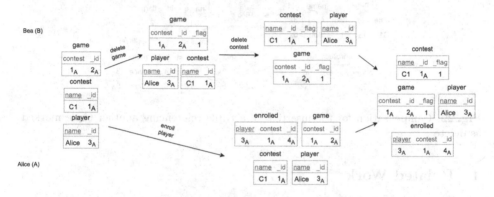

Fig. 20. Synql merging when game and contest are deleted at replica B.

In the second case, the compensation marks all tuples referenced by the new insertion as non-deleted, if those tuples are still present in the database state, meaning that they have been restored by a previous merging process. For example, if we perform an insertion where we enroll Bob to the same contest as Alice, we will end up in a state where the contest is compensated (delete flag incremented by one) as it is referenced by the new enrolled tuple. This situation is illustrated in Fig. 22. Note that, if more than one of the previously mentioned compensation cases happen consecutively at the same replica, compensation is only applied once.

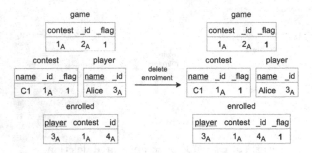

Fig. 21. Compensation for the scenario in Fig. 20

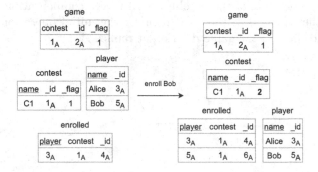

Fig. 22. Compensation for the insertion of a tuple referencing another tuple marked as delete

4   Related Work

Several coordination-less approaches, such as AQL [17], CRR [24] and IPA [5], have been designed to allow asynchronous work on databases. However, AQL and CRR fail to provide Strong Eventual Consistency and all of them fail to preserve the combined effect of operations' intent in complex scenarios.

AQL [17] is a database system that enables programmers to mitigate SQL consistency when possible. It is a preventive technique which allows application developers to choose between various semantics (no concurrency, update-wins, delete-wins) in order to avoid constraint violation in an update-delete scenario. For the no concurrency semantic, AQL uses multi-level locks in shared or exclusive mode to regulate the concurrent execution of actions in its databases [4,17]. Therefore, this method employs coordination in environments where strict consistency is required [17]. Moreover, the update-wins and delete-wins semantics frequently result in scenarios where the original operation intent is compromised (Fig. 11).

CRR [24] is a database management system which resolves constraint violation, without coordination, by combining the concept of causal length, an abstraction used to identify the causality between various updates, with a timestamp for each row in the database. In face of a conflict, the application undoes the newest operation causing the violation by incrementing its causal length by one and rolls back to the previous state. If the causal length is odd, then the action has been performed and included in the final state. If the causal length is even and different than 0, the action has been undone and is not taken into account in the final state [24].

IPA [5] is a database management system method which aims to preserve applications' invariants under weak consistency without impacting their availability and their latency. Rather than relying on coordination to prevent concurrency, this approach enables concurrent execution of operations and utilizes conflict resolution policies to guarantee a deterministic outcome (given the concurrently executing operations) while preserving invariants. However, these resolution and compensation techniques often lead to situation where the initial operation intent is broken (Fig. 10).

Synql achieves coordination-less replication while maintaining Strong Eventual Consistency. It provides support and compensation in face of constraint violations while preserving the combined effect of operations' intent.

5   Conclusions

We proposed a new approach called Synql for replicating relations and maintaining integrity constraints in face of concurrent modifications. In contrast to previous approaches, our proposal enforces Strong Eventual Consistency and respects combined effect of operations' intent in complex scenarios. Its replicated state consists of the composition of *CRDT* primitives. The state of the database is computed from the replicated state by deterministically resolving all integrity violations. Local modifications are compensated in a way that ensures the preservation of combined effect of operations' intent. The implementation is available at https://github.com/coast-team/synql.

References

1. Almeida, P.S., Shoker, A., Baquero, C.: Delta state replicated data types. J. Parallel Distrib. Comput. **111**, 162–173 (2018). https://doi.org/10.1016/j.jpdc.2017.08.003
2. Bailis, P., Fekete, A., Franklin, M.J., Ghodsi, A., Hellerstein, J.M., Stoica, I.: Feral concurrency control: an empirical investigation of modern application integrity. In: Proceedings of the 2015 ACM SIGMOD International Conference on Management of Data. SIGMOD 2015, Association for Computing Machinery, New York, NY, USA (2015). https://doi.org/10.1145/2723372.2737784
3. Bailis, P., Fekete, A.D., Franklin, M.J., Ghodsi, A., Hellerstein, J.M., Stoica, I.: Coordination avoidance in database systems. Proceedings of the VLDB Endowment **8**(3), 185–196 (2014). https://doi.org/10.14778/2735508.2735509
4. Balegas, V., et al.: Putting consistency back into eventual consistency. In: Proceedings of the Tenth European Conference on Computer Systems, pp. 1–16. EuroSys 2015 (2015). https://doi.org/10.1145/2741948.2741972

5. Balegas, V., Duarte, S., Ferreira, C., Rodrigues, R., Preguiça, N.M.: IPA: invariant-preserving applications for weakly consistent replicated databases. Proc. VLDB Endowment **12**(4), 404–418 (2018). https://doi.org/10.14778/3297753.3297760
6. Baquero, C., Almeida, P.S., Cunha, A., Ferreira, C.: Composition in state-based replicated data types. Bull. Eur. Assoc. Theor. Comput. Sci. **123** (2017). http://eatcs.org/beatcs/index.php/beatcs/article/view/507
7. Brewer, E.A.: Towards robust distributed systems (abstract). In: Proceedings of the Nineteenth Annual ACM Symposium on Principles of Distributed Computing, PODC 2000 (2000). https://doi.org/10.1145/343477.343502
8. Corbett, J.C., et al.: Spanner: Google's globally distributed database. ACM Trans. Comput. Syst. **31**(3) (2013). https://doi.org/10.1145/2491245
9. DeCandia, G., et al.: Dynamo: Amazon's highly available key-value store. In: Proceedings of Twenty-First ACM SIGOPS Symposium on Operating Systems Principles, SOSP 2007 (2007). https://doi.org/10.1145/1294261.1294281
10. Fox, A., Brewer, E.: Harvest, yield, and scalable tolerant systems. In: Proceedings of the Seventh Workshop on Hot Topics in Operating Systems, pp. 174–178, March 1999. https://doi.org/10.1109/HOTOS.1999.798396
11. Gilbert, S., Lynch, N.: Brewer's conjecture and the feasibility of consistent, available, partition-tolerant web services. ACM SIGACT News **33**(2), 51–59 (2002). https://doi.org/10.1145/564585.564601
12. Johnson, P.R., Thomas, R.: Maintenance of duplicate databases, January 1975. https://doi.org/10.17487/RFC0677
13. Kleppmann, M., Wiggins, A., van Hardenberg, P., McGranaghan, M.: Local-first software: you own your data, in spite of the cloud. In: Masuhara, H., Petricek, T. (eds.) Proceedings of the 2019 ACM SIGPLAN International Symposium on New Ideas, New Paradigms, and Reflections on Programming and Software. Onward! 2019 (2019). https://doi.org/10.1145/3359591.3359737
14. Kulkarni, S.S., Demirbas, M., Madappa, D., Avva, B., Leone, M.: Logical physical clocks. In: Proceedings of the 18th International Conference on Principles of Distributed Systems, OPODIS 2014 (2014). https://doi.org/10.1007/978-3-319-14472-6_2
15. Lakshman, A., Malik, P.: Cassandra: A decentralized structured storage system. ACM SIGOPS Oper. Syst. Rev. **44**(2), 35–40 (2010). https://doi.org/10.1145/1773912.1773922
16. Li, C., Porto, D., Clement, A., Gehrke, J., Preguiça, N.M., Rodrigues, R.: Making geo-replicated systems fast as possible, consistent when necessary. In: Thekkath, C., Vahdat, A. (eds.) Proceedings of the 10th USENIX Symposium on Operating Systems Design and Implementation, OSDI 2012 (2012). https://doi.org/10.5555/2387880.2387906
17. Lopes, P., et al.: Antidote SQL: relaxed when possible, strict when necessary (2019). http://arxiv.org/abs/1902.03576
18. Shapiro, M., Preguiça, N.M., Baquero, C., Zawirski, M.: Conflict-free replicated data types. In: Proceedings of the 13th International Symposium on Stabilization, Safety, and Security of Distributed Systems, SSS 2011 (2011). https://doi.org/10.1007/978-3-642-24550-3_29
19. Stonebraker, M., Madden, S., Abadi, D.J., Harizopoulos, S., Hachem, N., Helland, P.: The end of an architectural era: (it's time for a complete rewrite). In: Proceedings of the 33rd International Conference on Very Large Data Bases, VLDB 2007 (2007). https://doi.org/10.5555/1325851.1325981

20. Sumbaly, R., Kreps, J., Gao, L., Feinberg, A., Soman, C., Shah, S.: Serving large-scale batch computed data with project voldemort. In: Proceedings of the 10th USENIX Conference on File and Storage Technologies, FAST 2012, USENIX Association (2012). https://doi.org/10.5555/2208461.2208479
21. Thomson, A., Diamond, T., Weng, S.C., Ren, K., Shao, P., Abadi, D.J.: Calvin: fast distributed transactions for partitioned database systems. In: Proceedings of the 2012 ACM SIGMOD International Conference on Management of Data, SIGMOD 2012 (2012). https://doi.org/10.1145/2213836.2213838
22. Tu, S., Zheng, W., Kohler, E., Liskov, B., Madden, S.: Speedy transactions in multicore in-memory databases. In: Proceedings of the Twenty-Fourth ACM Symposium on Operating Systems Principles, SOSP 2013 (2013). https://doi.org/10.1145/2517349.2522713
23. Yu, W., Elvinger, V., Ignat, C.L.: A generic undo support for state-based CRDTS. In: Felber, P., Friedman, R., Gilbert, S., Miller, A. (eds.) Proceedings of the 23rd International Conference on Principles of Distributed Systems, OPODIS 2019 (2019). https://doi.org/10.4230/LIPIcs.OPODIS.2019.14
24. Yu, W., Ignat, C.L.: Conflict-free replicated relations for multi-synchronous database management at edge. In: Proceedings of the IEEE International Conference on Smart Data Services, SMDS 2020 (2020). https://doi.org/10.1109/SMDS49396.2020.00021

Encryption as a Service: A Review of Architectures and Taxonomies

Amir Javadpour[1]([✉]) [ID], Forough Ja'fari[2] [ID], and Tarik Taleb[3] [ID]

[1] ICTFICIAL Oy, Espoo, Finland
a.javadpour87@gmail.com
[2] Department of Computer Engineering, Sharif University of Technology,
Tehran, Iran
[3] Faculty of Electrical Engineering and Information Technology, Ruhr University
Bochum, Bochum, Germany

Abstract. Due to the rise of Internet of Things networks, targeting vulnerabilities related to the limitation of resources in devices has increased. Therefore, it is necessary to delegate encryption services to cloud and fog platforms. Encryption as a Service (EaaS) provides all cryptographic services to end-users to help them cope with their limited resources and processing capabilities. This paper reviews the existing research on EaaS platforms and categorizes them based on their underlying encryption algorithm types. We also introduce different EaaS architectures based on the location of the main components. To our knowledge, none of the existing surveys in this field have covered the aforementioned features.

Keywords: Internet of things (IoT) · Encryption as a Service
(EaaS) · Cloud/Edge computing · Full Cloud Fog architecture

1 Introduction

Cyberattacks are growing and improving daily, making researchers design and deploy mitigation activities. One of these activities is cryptography [7,8,11]. In previous decades, the cryptography processes were handled by the single remote servers or the end-devices themselves. However, due to the limitations in device resources in Internet of Things (IoT) devices, and the risk of being a single point of failure when single servers are used, the researchers move toward ways of providing cryptography services in a distributed environment [8,20]. Hence, Encryption as a Service (EaaS) emerged.

Several surveys have reviewed the research on EaaS [10,13]. However, they do not cover recent works as they are relatively old, and none have discussed the advantages and disadvantages of different architectures of EaaS. This paper, first, gives the background concept of EaaS, then explains the various architec-

© IFIP International Federation for Information Processing 2024
Published by Springer Nature Switzerland AG 2024
R. Martins and M. Selimi (Eds.): DAIS 2024, LNCS 14677, pp. 36–44, 2024.
https://doi.org/10.1007/978-3-031-62638-8_3

tures of an EaaS platform, and finally, categorizes the reviewed research based on the underlying encryption type. The paper in question has made several noteworthy contributions to the field of EaaS. Firstly, it has undertaken a review of a broad range of research studies related to EaaS, highlighting and discussing the various challenges faced in the field. Secondly, the authors have identified four general architectures for EaaS, and have categorized the existing research work based on these architectures. This has helped provide a better understanding of the different approaches taken in the field of EaaS. Lastly, the authors have presented a categorization of EaaS platforms based on the types of encryption they utilize. This has been particularly useful in identifying the encryption techniques employed in EaaS platforms and has helped assess their efficacy and suitability for different use cases.

2   Background

Making data only readable by legitimate users is called cryptography. The raw data and a single or a pair of keys are passed to the encryption algorithm, and a ciphertext is obtained. The ciphertext can be converted to the original raw data during decryption only when the related key(s) are available. Therefore, the data owner can share the associated keys for decrypting data with only those permitted to read [1].

Providing cryptography services and all of the main processes as a cloud service is called EaaS. All the EaaS platforms do not have the same components; however, we can say that the main components, which can also be called as crypto components, are (1) general manager, (2) key manager, (3) encryptor, and (4) decryptor. The general manager is responsible for managing a request from when it is received until it is responded to. The processes under its management contain choosing an appropriate key manager, encryptor, or decryptor for a request, and checking users' authorities. The key manager components create appropriate keys and handle all the related processes. Finally, the encryptor and the decryptor components receive related keys and perform encryption and decryption on a given data. The sequence diagram shown in Fig. 1 indicates how different components communicate to serve a cryptography request.

We can see in Fig. 1, that an end-device, which is the data owner, wants to share it on a public cloud, but safely, only specific devices can read. In Step 1, the raw data and the algorithm type are sent to the general manager component. Once received, the general management component checks the status of available key managers, selects one, and sends the algorithm type toward it (Step 2). When the selected key manager receives the algorithm type, the keys are generated based on it and sent back to the general manager (Step 3). Then again, the general manager selects an appropriate encryptor, and sends the raw data and the generated key(s) toward it through step 4. When the encryption process

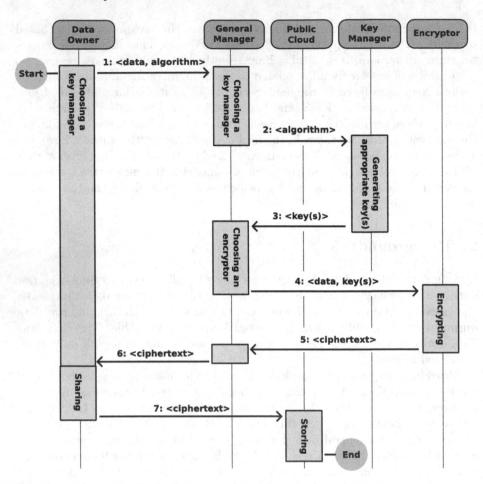

Fig. 1. A diagram illustrating the sequence of events in a simple EaaS system designed for sharing encrypted information. This Figure shows how different components communicate to serve a cryptography request. The data owner shares the raw data and algorithm type with the general manager, who selects a key manager to generate the keys. Then, an encryptor encrypts the data and sends it back to the owner. Other devices can access the data if they have permission. A decryptor component is involved in the process of reading the encrypted data. Backup crypto components are sometimes used to avoid a single point of failure.

is complete, the encrypted data (i.e., ciphertext) is sent back to the general manager and forwarded to the data owner (Step 5 and Step 6). The data owner can now share the encrypted data on the public cloud in Step 7. When another device attempts to access shared data on the public cloud, the encrypted data is sent to the general manager, which follows similar steps if authorized to access it. The only difference is that a decryptor component is now involved instead of an encryptor. It must be noted that not to have a single point of failure, and some platforms use backup crypto components too [22].

3   EaaS Architectures

Different architectures have been proposed for EaaS platforms. The location of crypto components varies in other architectures. These three layers can host the entities: (1) device layer, (2) cloud layer, and (3) fog layer. The devices on the device layer have limited resources and cannot execute complex processes. The nodes on the cloud layer are physical or virtual systems that function as cloud nodes. These nodes are rich resources, can do complex processes, and offer big storage spaces to users. The nodes on the fog layer are near the edge and are considered intermediary nodes. We can categorize the EaaS architectures currently proposed by the researchers into four categories based on the location of their crypto components. We use the term "Full" to indicate that none of these components are located on the device layer, and the cloud and fog layers fully handle the processes. And on the other hand, the term "Half" refers to the architectures that use the end-devices as part of the cryptography process. These categories are as follows [9]:

- **Full-Cloud:** This architecture contains only the cloud layer. This means there is almost no limitation in the resources, and the cryptography service can serve a wide range of end-devices. The EaaS platforms based on the full-cloud architecture are easy to implement, and the request acceptance ratio is high due to having almost no constraints on resources. However, as the included nodes are located on the cloud layer, there may be a significant delay in response.
- **Half-Cloud:** This architecture contains device and cloud layers. The end devices must have the least required resources when a platform works based on the half-cloud architecture. This is because these devices are also involved in some cryptography processes. However, most platforms with the half-cloud architecture do not make end-devices perform complicated tasks. As a result, only simple ones are done by the device layer.
- **Half-Fog:** The half-fog architecture includes two layers, which are the device and the fog layer. The devices that want to be served by EaaS platforms under this architecture must have at least a specific amount of resources. In some platforms, the end-devices under "Half" architectures, the fog nodes only decide the type of cryptography algorithm, and generate the related key(s). The end-devices perform the other processes by themselves [4].
- **Half-Cloud-Fog architecture:** In this architecture, the EaaS platform's key components are distributed across three layers. This architecture is a hybrid of half-cloud and half-fog. Not all EaaS platforms in the "Half" category require end-devices to perform cryptographic tasks. Some platforms ask for only powerful devices to do them [24].

A summary of EaaS architectures and the researchers working on them are presented in Table 1

Table 1. A comparison of different EaaS architectures and the research on each type.

Architecture	Full-Cloud	Half-Cloud	Half-Fog	Half-Cloud-Fog
Scheme	General Manager / Key Manager / Encryptor/Decryptor — Cloud Layer / Fog Layer / Device Layer	General Manager / Key Manager / Encryptor/Decryptor — Cloud Layer / Fog Layer / Encryptor/Decryptor — Device Layer	Cloud Layer / General Manager / Key Manager — Fog Layer / Encryptor/Decryptor — Device Layer	General Manager — Cloud Layer / Key Manager — Fog Layer / Encryptor/Decryptor — Device Layer
Features	High compatibility but high delay	Medium to high compatibility but medium to high delay	Low delay but medium compatibility	Medium to low delay but medium compatibility
Reference	[3, 23, 21, 5, 17]	[22]	[4, 12]	[24]

4   Categorized EaaS Encryption Types

An EaaS platform can offer various types of cryptographic services, which can be categorized as follows:

– **Attribute-Based EaaS (ABEaaS):** In normal encryption, the cryptography features do not change in different cases. However, ABEaaS provides a way to apply these changes based on user or environment attributes. The ABEaaS platform proposed by [4] tries to cover as much end-devices as possible by suggesting the algorithms that the end-devices can perform.
– **Homomorphic EaaS (HEaaS):** Users may sometimes require specific operations to access encrypted data, but may hesitate to do so due to privacy concerns. Homomorphic Encryption as a Service (HEaaS) is a viable solution. A recent research paper [5] presents an innovative HEaaS offering specializing in cryptography services for encrypting and decrypting images. With this HEaaS solution, users can perform operations on encrypted images without needing to decrypt them, thus ensuring the privacy and security of the data owner's information.
– **Searchable EaaS (SEaaS):** This type of encryption is for situations, where there is a need for searching a keyword in encrypted data without decrypting it. A sample SEaaS is proposed by [18] for British telecommunication cloud, making keywords with typo errors searchable. Searching for a specific keyword within encrypted data may be necessary without decrypting the entire dataset in certain scenarios. This is where a particular type of encryption comes into play. The encryption method allows searching keywords within encrypted data while keeping it secure. An example of such a service is the SEaaS proposed by [18] for the British telecommunication cloud. This service not

only enables the searching of keywords within encrypted data, but also allows for typos to be accounted for during the search process. This approach ensures that the data remains secure, allowing for efficient and accurate searchability.
- **Proxy Re-EaaS (PREaaS):** This encryption type is for situations, where two parties want to share encrypted data, but without sharing the keys used for decrypting it. Some examples of these situations are when emails are forwarded to others and when content is distributed. proposes a PREaaS cite2019prasa to protect the data shared between the components of smart grids. In this platform, the location of the proxy is changed to find which one has the best performance. In this scenario, it becomes necessary for two parties to share encrypted data without sharing the keys used for decrypting it. This is where a specific encryption type comes into play. For instance, this encryption type is quite valuable when emails are forwarded to others or when a particular content is distributed. The primary goal of this platform is to safeguard the data shared between the various components of smart grids. To achieve this, the location of the proxy is altered to locate the one with the best performance. This way, the data remains secure while ensuring optimal performance.
- **Quantum EaaS (QEaaS):** In this encryption type, the concepts of quantum mechanics are used for performing cryptography. When data is encrypted using this technique, the receiver can find out if illegal parties read it because the photons are changed when they are read. proposes sample work in this field cite2021qucras, where a QEaaS is designed for applying security to the communications between aerial vehicles. This QEaaS contains five layers, one for gathering data, another for presenting the physical devices, one layer for performing quantum encryption, the fourth one for communications, and the last one as the storing layer. In a recent research paper, [14] proposed a QEaaS system to enhance communication security between aerial vehicles. This QEaaS system comprises five key layers that provide a comprehensive security solution. The first layer gathers the necessary data, while the second is dedicated to the physical devices used in the communication process. The third layer is the quantum encryption layer, which applies advanced encryption techniques to ensure data confidentiality. The fourth layer handles the communication process, and the last layer stores the data securely. Implementing this QEaaS system in aerial vehicles makes it possible to ensure that all communication is secure and protected against any potential threats. This can be especially important when sensitive information must be transmitted between aerial vehicles.

A summary of the research in each category is presented in Table 2. There is another category in this table, called General EaaS (GEaaS) for presenting other types of EaaS than those mentioned.

Table 2. A summary of Review of Research on Varied Encryption types

Ref	Type	Year	Architecture	Description
[3]	ABEaaS	2017	Full-Cloud	Splitting ABEaaS into multiple sub-services.
[21]		2021	Full-Cloud	Considering users' identity as the attributes.
[4]		2022	Half-Fog	Covering more devices by selecting optimal features.
[5]	HEaaS	2020	Full-Cloud	Serving cryptography services for images.
[15]		2023	Full-Cloud	Providing role-based HEaaS.
[18]	SEaaS	2019	Half-Cloud	Handling typo errors in SEaaS searches.
[19]		2020	Half-Cloud	Improving SEaaS using multiple threads for searching.
[6]		2023	Full-Cloud	Improving SEaaS by probabilistic encryption.
[16]	PREaaS	2019	Full-Cloud	Improving PREaaS by changing the proxy location.
[17]		2021	Full-Cloud	Using elliptic curves to improve PREaaS.
[12]	QEaaS	2019	Half-Fog	A testbed deploying QEaaS for beyond 5G networks.
[14]		2021	Full-Cloud	A QEaaS platform for protecting aerial vehicles.
[24]	GEaaS	2019	Half-Cloud-Fog	Protecting smart substations with Knapsack algorithm.
[2]		2020	Full-Cloud	Changing encryption configurations using an agent.
[23]		2021	Full-Cloud	Protecting traffic between Kubernetes pods

5 Conclusion

This paper presents an all-inclusive summary of various EaaS platforms suggested by researchers in the respective fields. We have categorized their architecture into four classes, namely, Full-Cloud, Fog, Hybrid, and Edge. Additionally, we have investigated these platforms based on the encryption type they provide, such as symmetric, asymmetric, and homomorphic encryption. However, EaaS platforms face two significant challenges: the availability of the components and the trade-off between the number of covered devices and the service performance. To address these issues, researchers have proposed various solutions, including implementing a Full-Cloud-Fog architecture that combines the benefits of both centralized and distributed architectures. Furthermore, utilizing machine learning approaches such as deep learning and reinforcement learning can also enhance the performance of EaaS platforms. These approaches can help optimize the encryption algorithms and protocols and predict the components' availability.

Acknowledgment. This research work is partially supported by the European Union's Horizon Europe research and innovation program HORIZON-JU-SNS-2022 under the RIGOUROUS project (Grant No. 101095933). The paper reflects only the authors' views. The Commission is not responsible for any use that may be made of the information it contains.

References

1. Al-Shabi, M.: A survey on symmetric and asymmetric cryptography algorithms in information security. Int. J. Sci. Res. Publ. (IJSRP) **9**(3), 576–589 (2019)
2. Ateeq, K., Pradhan, M.R., Mago, B., Ghazal, T.: Encryption as a service for multi-cloud environment. Int. J. Adv. Res. Eng. Technol. (IJARET) **11**(7), 622–628 (2020)

3. Blömer, J., Günther, P., Krummel, V., Löken, N.: Attribute-based encryption as a service for access control in large-scale organizations. In: Imine, A., Fernandez, J.M., Marion, J.-Y., Logrippo, L., Garcia-Alfaro, J. (eds.) FPS 2017. LNCS, vol. 10723, pp. 3–17. Springer, Cham (2018). https://doi.org/10.1007/978-3-319-75650-9_1

4. Deb, P.K., Mukherjee, A., Misra, S.: CEaaS: constrained encryption-as-a-service in fog-enabled IoT. IEEE Internet Things J. **9**, 19803–19810 (2022)

5. Ibtihal, M., Hassan, N.: Homomorphic encryption as a service for outsourced images in mobile cloud computing environment. In: Cryptography: Breakthroughs in Research and Practice, pp. 316–330. IGI Global (2020)

6. Ihtesham, M., et al.: Privacy preserving and serverless homomorphic-based searchable encryption as a service (SEaaS). IEEE Access **11**, 115204–115218 (2023)

7. Javadpour, A., Ja'fari, F., Taleb, T., Shojafar, M., Benzaïd, C.: A comprehensive survey on cyber deception techniques to improve honeypot performance. Comput. Secur. **140**, 103792 (2024)

8. Javadpour, A., Ja'fari, F., Taleb, T., Shojafar, M., Yang, B.: SCEMA: an SDN-oriented cost-effective edge-based MTD approach. IEEE Trans. Inf. Forensics Secur. **18**, 667–682 (2022)

9. Javadpour, A., Ja'fari, F., Taleb, T., Zhao, Y., Bin, Y., Benzaïd, C.: Encryption as a service for IoT: opportunities, challenges and solutions. IEEE Internet Things J **11**, 7525–7558 (2023)

10. Olanrewaju, R.F., Islam, T., Khalifa, O.O., Anwar, F., Pampori, B.R.: Cryptography as a service (CaaS): quantum cryptography for secure cloud computing. Indian J. Sci. Technol. **10**(7), 1–6 (2017)

11. Patel, A., et al.: Safeguarding the IoT: taxonomy, security solutions, and future research opportunities. Secur. Priv. **7**(2), e354 (2024)

12. Raddo, T.R., Rommel, S., Land, V., Okonkwo, C., Monroy, I.T.: Quantum data encryption as a service on demand: Eindhoven QKD network testbed. In: 2019 21st International Conference on Transparent Optical Networks (ICTON), pp. 1–5. IEEE (2019)

13. Rahimi, N., Reed, J.J., Gupta, B.: On the significance of cryptography as a service. J. Inf. Secur. **9**(4), 242–256 (2018)

14. Ralegankar, V.K., et al.: Quantum cryptography-as-a-service for secure UAV communication: applications, challenges, and case study. IEEE Access **10**, 1475–1492 (2021)

15. Saxena, U.R., Alam, T.: Role-based access using partial homomorphic encryption for securing cloud data. Int. J. Syst. Assur. Eng. Manage. **14**(3), 950–966 (2023)

16. Sbai, A., Drocourt, C., Dequen, G.: Pre as a service within smart grid city. In: 16th International Conference on Security and Cryptography, pp. 394–401. SCITEPRESS-Science and Technology Publications (2019)

17. Sbai, A., Drocourt, C., Dequen, G.: Cloud file sharing using PREaaS. EHEI J. Sci. Technol. **1**(2), 52–63 (2021)

18. Tahir, S., Ruj, S., Sajjad, A., Rajarajan, M.: Fuzzy keywords enabled ranked searchable encryption scheme for a public cloud environment. Comput. Commun. **133**, 102–114 (2019)

19. Tahir, S., Steponkus, L., Ruj, S., Rajarajan, M., Sajjad, A.: A parallelized disjunctive query based searchable encryption scheme for big data. Futur. Gener. Comput. Syst. **109**, 583–592 (2020)

20. Thabit, F., Can, O., Aljahdali, A.O., Al-Gaphari, G.H., Alkhzaimi, H.A.: A comprehensive literature survey of cryptography algorithms for improving the IoT security. Internet of Things **22**, 100759 (2023)

21. Unal, D., Al-Ali, A., Catak, F.O., Hammoudeh, M.: A secure and efficient internet of things cloud encryption scheme with forensics investigation compatibility based on identity-based encryption. Futur. Gener. Comput. Syst. **125**, 433–445 (2021)

22. Xu, R., Joshi, J.B.: Enabling attribute based encryption as an internet service. In: 2016 IEEE 2nd International Conference on Collaboration and Internet Computing (CIC), pp. 417–425. IEEE (2016)

23. Yang, B., Zhang, F., Khan, S.U.: An encryption-as-a-service architecture on cloud native platform. In: 2021 International Conference on Computer Communications and Networks (ICCCN), pp. 1–7. IEEE (2021)

24. Zhang, H., Qin, B., Tu, T., Guo, Z., Gao, F., Wen, Q.: An adaptive encryption-as-a-service architecture based on fog computing for real-time substation communications. IEEE Trans. Industr. Inf. **16**(1), 658–668 (2019)

Compact Storage of Data Streams in Mobile Devices

Rémy Raes[1]([✉]), Olivier Ruas[2]([✉]), Adrien Luxey-Bitri[1]([✉]),
and Romain Rouvoy[1]([✉])

[1] Inria, University of Lille, CNRS, UMR 9189 CRIStAL, Villeneuve d'Ascq, France
{remy.raes,adrien.luxey,romain.rouvoy}@inria.fr
[2] Pathway, Villeneuve d'Ascq, France
olivier.ruas@gmail.com

Abstract. Data streams produced by mobile devices, such as smartphones, offer highly valuable sources of information to build ubiquitous services. However, the diversity of embedded sensors and the resulting data deluge makes it impractical to provision such services directly on mobiles, due to their constrained storage capacity, communication bandwidth and processing power. Unfortunately, the improving hardware capabilities of devices are unlikely to resolve these structural issues. We, therefore, believe that mobile data management systems should, instead, handle data streams efficiently and compactly, to provision services directly at the edge, while accounting for the limits of existing assets and network infrastructures. This paper introduces the FLI framework, which leverages a piece-wise linear approximation technique to capture compact representations of data streams in mobile devices. Our experiments, performed on Android and iOS devices, show that FLI outperforms the state of the art both in memory footprint and I/O throughput. Our Flutter implementation of FLI can store stream datasets in mobile devices, which is a prerequisite to processing big data from ubiquitous devices *in situ*.

1 Introduction

With the advent of smartphones and more generally the *Internet of Things* (IoT), ubiquitous devices are mainstream in our societies and widely deployed at the edge of networks. Such constrained devices are not only consuming data and services, such as content streaming, restaurant recommendations or more generally *Location-Based Services* (LBSs), but are also key producers of data streams by leveraging a wide variety of embedded sensors that capture the surrounding environment of end-users, including their daily routines. The data deluge generated by a connected user is potentially tremendous: according to preliminary experiments, a smartphone can generate approximately 2 pairs of *Global Positioning System* (GPS) samples and 476 triplets of accelerometer samples per second, resulting in more than 172,800 location and 41,126,400 acceleration samples daily.

In this context, the storage and processing of such data streams in mobile devices are challenges that cannot only be addressed by assuming that the hardware capabilities will keep increasing. In particular, sustainability issues call for

R. Martins and M. Selimi (Eds.): DAIS 2024, LNCS 14677, pp. 45–61, 2024.
https://doi.org/10.1007/978-3-031-62638-8_4

increasing the lifespan of legacy devices, thus postponing their replacement. This implies that software-defined solutions are required to leverage the shortenings of hardware resources.

This paper, therefore, demonstrates that modeling data streams successfully address these device-level storage & processing challenges. More specifically, to address the storage challenge, we introduce *Fast Linear Interpolation* (FLI): a novel algorithm leveraging a *Piece-wise Linear Approximation* (PLA) technique to model and store data streams under memory constraints. Figure 1 illustrates FLI's behavior: to capture the trajectory displayed on Fig. 1a, FLI does not store raw data samples (Figs. 1b and 1d) but, instead, models their evolution as linear interpolations (Figs. 1c and 1e) —thus offering a much bigger storage capacity at the cost of a controlled approximation error.

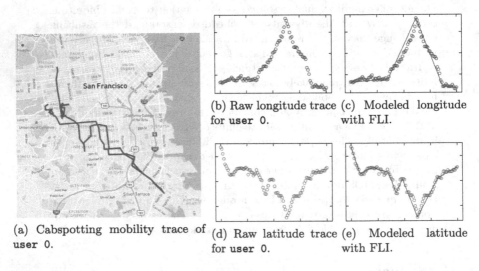

(a) Cabspotting mobility trace of user 0.

(b) Raw longitude trace for user 0.

(c) Modeled longitude with FLI.

(d) Raw latitude trace for user 0.

(e) Modeled latitude with FLI.

Fig. 1. FLI compacts any location stream as a sequence of segments.

In the following, we first discuss the related works (Sect. 2), before diving into the details of FLI (Sect. 3). We then present our experimental setup (Sect. 4) and the results we obtained (Sect. 5). Finally, we discuss the limitations of our approach (Sect. 6), before concluding (Sect. 7).

2   Related Work

Overcoming the memory constraints of mobile devices to store data streams usually implies the integration of efficient temporal databases. To take the example of Android: few databases are available, such as SQLITE and its derivative DRIFT [3], the cloud-supported Firebase [20], the NoSQL HIVE, and OBJECT-BOX [5]. The situation is similar on iOS.

Relational databases (e.g., SQL) are typically designed for *OnLine Transactional Processing* (OLTP) and *OnLine Analytical Processing* (OLAP) workloads, which widely differ from time-series workloads. In the latter, reads are mostly contiguous (as opposed to the random-read tendency of OLTP); writes are most often inserts (not updates) and typically target the most recent time ranges. OLAP is designed to store big data workloads to compute analytical statistics, while not putting the emphasis on read or write performances. Finally, in temporal workloads, it is unlikely to process writes & reads in the same single transaction [21].

Time series databases (TSDB). Despite these deep differences, several relational databases offer support for temporal data with industry-ready performance— *e.g.,* TIMESCALEDB [9] is a middleware that exposes temporal functionalities atop a relational POSTGRESQL foundation. INFLUXDB [10] is one of the most widely used temporal databases. Unfortunately, when facing memory constraints, its retention policy prevents the storage from scaling in time: the oldest samples are dumped to make room for the new ones. Furthermore, on mobile, memory shortages often cause the operating system to kill the TSDB process to free the memory, which is opposed to the very concept of in-memory databases.

Moving Objects Databases (MOD). Location data storage is an issue that has also been studied in the MOD community, where a central authority merges trajectory data from several sensors in real-time. To optimize storage and communication costs, it does not store the raw location data, but rather trajectory approximations. *Linear Dead Reckoning* (LDR) [23] limits data exchange between sensors and server by sending new location samples only when a predefined *accuracy bound* ϵ (in meters) is exceeded. A mobility prediction vector is additionally shared every time a location sample is sent. Even so, this class of solutions requires temporarily storing modeled locations to ensure they fit the ϵ bound and exclusively focuses on modeling location data streams, while we aim at storing any type of real-valued stream.

Modeling Data Streams. While being discrete, the streams sampled by sensors represent inherently continuous signals. Data modeling does not only allow important memory consumption gains, but also flattens sensors' noise, and enables extrapolation between measurements. In particular, *Piece-wise Linear Approximation* (PLA) is used to model the data as successive affine functions. An intuitive way to do linear approximation is to apply a bottom-up segmentation: each pair of consecutive points is connected by interpolations; the less significant contiguous interpolations are merged, as long as the obtained interpolations introduce no error above a given threshold. The bottom-up approach has low complexity, but usually requires an offline approach to consider all the points at once. The *Sliding Window And Bottom-up* (SWAB) algorithm [11], however, is an online approach that uses a sliding window to buffer the latest samples on which a bottom-up approach is applied. EMSWAB [2] improves the sliding window by adding several samples at the same time instead of one. Instead of interpolation, linear regression can also be used to model the samples reported by IoT sensors [8]. For example, GREYCAT [13] adopts polynomial regressions with higher degrees to further compress the data. Unfortunately, none of those works have been implemented on mobile devices to date.

SPRINTZ [4] proposes a mobile lossless compression scheme for multi-modal integer data streams, along with a comparison of other compression algorithms. They target streaming of the compressed data to a centralized location from IoT devices with minimal resources. This work is orthogonal to ours, as FLI intends to model floating-point unimodal streams on one's devices for further local computation, instead of streaming it to a third-party server.

Closer to our work, FSW [12] and the SHRINKINGCONE algorithm [6] attempt to maximize the length of a segment while satisfying a given error threshold, using the same property used in FLI. FSW is not a streaming algorithm as it considers the dataset as a whole, and does not support insertion. The SHRINK-INGCONE algorithm is a streaming greedy algorithm designed to approximate an index, mapping keys to positions: it only considers monotonic increasing functions and can produce disjoints segments. FLI models non-monotonic functions in a streaming fashion, while providing joint segments.

Limitations. To the best of our knowledge, state-of-the-art storage solutions for unbounded data streams either require storing raw data samples or triggering *a posteriori* data computations, which makes them unsuitable for mobile devices.

3   Storing Data Streams in the Small

3.1   Leveraging Piecewise Linear Approximations

To overcome the memory constraint of mobile devices, we claim that efficient temporal storage solutions must be ported onto ubiquitous environments. In particular, we advocate the use of data modeling, such as *Piece-wise Linear Approximation* (PLA) [8,11] or GREYCAT [13], to increase the storage capacity of mobile devices. Therefore, we introduce FLI, a time series modeling algorithm based on an iterative and continuous PLA to store approximate models of data streams on memory-constrained devices, instead of storing all the raw data samples as state-of-the-art temporal databases do. FLI models one-dimensional points (or samples) p as piece-wise linear segments (or interpolations) s. It enforces the following invariant: *all samples modeled by an interpolation maintain an error below the configuration parameter ϵ*. Its data structure $\mathcal{D}$ is composed of $i)$ a list of selected historical points $\mathcal{P}$, $ii)$ the latest segment's gradient α_M, and $iii)$ the two bounding gradients $\alpha_{\min}$ and $\alpha_{\max}$ used for insertion:

$$\mathcal{D} = (\mathcal{P}, \alpha_M, \alpha_{\min}, \alpha_{\max}), \text{ s.t.}$$

$$\mathcal{P} = [\ldots, p_i, p_{i+1}, \ldots, p_M] \subset \mathbb{R}^2 \ \& \ (\alpha_M, \alpha_{\min}, \alpha_{\max}) \in \mathbb{R}^3$$

Historical segments are captured as tuples of consecutive samples: $s_i = [p_i, p_{i+1}]$. The latest interpolation s_M takes the last inserted sample p_M as its origin and the gradient α_M as its slope, as depicted in Fig. 2. We first present how observed points are inserted, before explaining how reading a value is performed.

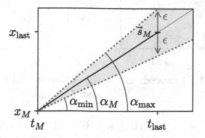

Fig. 2. A new FLI interpolation s_M begins with 2 samples: the point $p_M = (t_M, x_M)$ as origin, and the latest sample $p_{\text{last}} = (t_{\text{last}}, x_{\text{last}})$ as slope α_M. 2 bounding gradients $\alpha_{\min}$ and $\alpha_{\max}$ are derived from ϵ, and used to assert if future inserts fit s_M.

3.2 Inserting Data Samples

Data samples are inserted sequentially: the current interpolation is adjusted to fit new samples until it cannot satisfy the invariant. Upon insertion of a new sample p, the slope α of the segment $[p_M, p]$ is compared to the interval $[\alpha_{\min}, \alpha_{\max}]$. If it falls within (cf. Fig. 3), p is added to the current interpolation: $\alpha_{\min}$ and $\alpha_{\max}$ are updated to encompass p, α_M is updated to α (for reading), and the previous sample is dropped. If p is outside the interval (cf. Fig. 4), a new interpolation begins from the 2 last points.

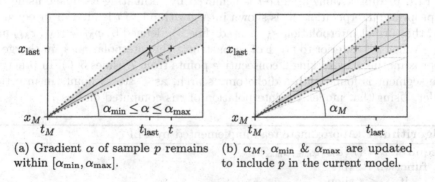

(a) Gradient α of sample p remains within $[\alpha_{\min}, \alpha_{\max}]$.

(b) α_M, $\alpha_{\min}$ & $\alpha_{\max}$ are updated to include p in the current model.

Fig. 3. When a new sample fits within $[\alpha_{\min}, \alpha_{\max}]$, it is added to the current model by updating $\alpha_{\min}$ and $\alpha_{\max}$. α_M is also updated for read queries (see Algorithm 1).

The value of ϵ has an important impact on the performances of FLI. If ϵ is too small, none of the inserted samples fits the current model at that time, thus initiating a new model each time. In that case, there will be one model per sample, imposing an important memory overhead. The resulting model overfits the data. On the other hand, if ϵ is too large, then all the inserted samples fit,

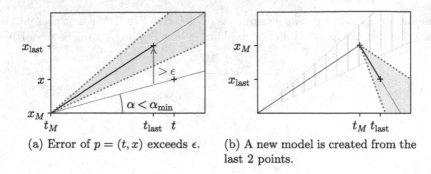

(a) Error of $p = (t, x)$ exceeds ϵ.

(b) A new model is created from the last 2 points.

Fig. 4. When an error $> \epsilon$ is reported, a new model is created using p_{last} as p_M.

and a single model is kept. While it is the best case memory-wise, the resulting model simply connects the first and last point and underfits the data.

As long as the newly inserted data samples fit the existing model, the memory footprint of FLI remains unchanged. This potentially unlimited storage capacity makes FLI a key asset for mobile devices, for example drastically increasing the storage capacity for user mobility traces. While FLI is designed for the modeling of univariate data streams, it straight-forwardly generalizes to multivariate data streams by combining several instances of FLI. We, therefore, claim that the use of FLI alleviates the memory constraint of mobile devices, hence opening new opportunities to process unbounded data streams locally.

3.3   Reading Data Streams

In FLI, reading a value at time t is achieved by estimating its image using the appropriate interpolation, as is shown in Algorithm 1. If t is ulterior or equal to t_M, the current interpolation s_M is used (line 3), defined by $p_M = (t_M, x_M)$ and α_M. When t is anterior to t_M, FLI reconstructs the interpolation s_i in charge of approximating t by picking 2 consecutive points from $\mathcal{P}$ (lines 5–6). In practice, the segment is found with a dichotomy search, as $\mathcal{P}$ stores points in insertion order. Using that model, the interpolation of t is computed on line 7.

Algorithm 1. Approximate read implemented by FLI

Require: $\mathcal{D} = (\mathcal{P}, \alpha_M, \alpha_{min}, \alpha_{max})$
1: **function** READ($t \in \mathbb{R}$)
2:     **if** $t_M \leq t$ **then**
3:         **return** $\alpha_M \times (t - t_M) + x_M$
4:     **end if**
5:     **select** i **s.t.** $((t_i, x_i), (t_{i+1}, x_{i+1})) \in \mathcal{P} \wedge t_i \leq t < t_{i+1}$
6:     $\alpha_i \leftarrow (x_{i+1} - x_i) / (t_{i+1} - t_i)$
7:     **return** $\alpha_i \times (t - t_i) + x_i$
8: **end function**

---

4   Experimental Setup

4.1   Key Performance Metrics

We consider state-of-the-art system metrics to evaluate the performance of FLI:

Memory Footprint. The key objective of FLI is to reduce the memory footprint required to store an unbounded stream of samples. We explore two metrics: *(i)* the number of 64-bit variables required by the model and *(ii)* the size of the model in the device memory. To do so, we compare the size of the persistent file with the size of the vanilla SQLITE database file. We consider the number of 64-bit variables as a device-agnostic estimation of the model footprint.

I/O Throughput. Another key system metric is the I/O throughput of the temporal databases. In particular, we measure how many write and read operations can be performed per second (IOPS).

4.2   Input Datasets and Parameter Tuning

FLI is data-agnostic: any data stream can be modeled using it (cf. Sect. 5.4). However, the ϵ parameter depends on the underlying data distribution. In the following, we propose a protocol to tune an ϵ value according to the modeled data stream. We use mobility traces as a representative example of data streams that can be stored and processed by modern mobile devices. In particular, we believe that mobility traces are a good candidate for FLI as the storage of sampled user locations may require a lot of storage space. A mobility trace is defined as an ordered sequence T of pairs (t, g) where t is a timestamp and g is a geolocation sample, a latitude-longitude pair for example. The trace is ordered in chronological order and we assume that reported timestamps are unique.

Location Datasets. CABSPOTTING [15] is a mobility dataset of 536 taxis in the San Francisco Bay Area. The data was collected during a month and is composed of 11 million records, for a total of 388 MB. PRIVAMOV [14] is a multi-sensors mobility dataset gathered during 15 months by 100 users around the city of Lyon, France. We use the full GPS dataset, which includes 156 million records, totaling 7.2 GB. Compared to CABSPOTTING, PRIVAMOV is a highly-dense mobility dataset.

Parameter Tuning. The choice of an ϵ value is of major importance and plays a central role in FLI's performances: a poorly-chosen value has a strong impact on FLI's underlying segments, either degrading modeled data quality or filling storage space up excessively. To find a compromise between the two, since the ϵ value is highly correlated to the modeled data, one has to *know* the data; more specifically, we advise studying data variation between consecutive values.

For example, in the context of location data, Fig. 5 characterizes—as a *Cumulative Distribution Function* (CDF)—the evolution of longitude and latitude samples for all the traces stored in the CABSPOTTING and PRIVAMOV datasets. In particular, we plot the CDF of the drift d observed between 2 consecutive values (x_1, y_1) and (x_2, y_2), which we compute as $d = |y_2 - y_1|/|x_2 - x_1|$. One can observe that CABSPOTTING and PRIVAMOV datasets report on a drift lower than 1×10^{-4} and 2×10^{-5} for 90% of the values, respectively. Furthermore, due to the high density of locations captured by PRIVAMOV, half of the drifts are equal to 0, meaning several consecutive longitudes or latitudes are unchanged.

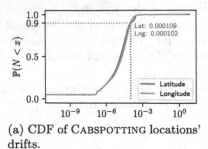

(a) CDF of CABSPOTTING locations' drifts.

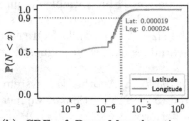

(b) CDF of PRIVAMOV locations' drifts.

Fig. 5. *Cumulative Distribution Function* (CDF) of latitude and longitude drifts of successive location samples in CABSPOTTING and PRIVAMOV datasets. One can observe that, from one location sample to the next, latitude or longitude deviations are small.

This preliminary analysis of both datasets highlights that mobility traces are highly relevant data streams for FLI, and demonstrates $\epsilon = 10^{-3}$ is a conservative choice to model location data. To automate the tuning of ϵ, FLI comes with a script that takes a sample input to report on candidate ϵ values to capture 90%, 95% and 99% of the sampled data. The following sections will focus on the evaluation of FLI on those datasets to study the benefits of adopting FLI to capture real-world metrics in mobile devices.

4.3   Storage Competitors

SQLITE is the state-of-the-art solution to persist and query large volumes of data on Android devices. SQLITE provides a lightweight relational database management system. SQLITE is not a temporal database, but is a convenient and standard way to store samples persistently on a mobile device. Insertions are atomic, so one may batch them to avoid one memory access per insertion.

Sliding-Window And Bottom-up (SWAB) [11] is a linear interpolation model. As FLI, the samples are represented by a list of linear models. In particular, reading a sample is achieved by iteratively going through the list of models until the corresponding one is found and then used to estimate the requested value. The bottom-up approach of SWAB starts by connecting every pair of consecutive samples and then iterates by merging the less significant pair of contiguous interpolations. This process is repeated until no more pairs can be merged without introducing an error higher than ϵ. Contrarily to FLI, this bottom-up approach is an offline one, requiring all the samples to be known. SWAB extends the bottom-up approach by buffering samples in a sliding window. New samples are inserted in the sliding window and then modeled using a bottom-up approach: whenever the window is full, the oldest model is kept and the captured samples are removed from the buffer.

One could expect that the bottom-up approach delivers more accurate models than the greedy FLI, even resulting in a slight reduction in the number of models and faster readings. On the other hand, sample insertion is more expensive than FLI due to the execution of the bottom-up approach when storing samples. Like FLI, SWAB ensures that reading stored samples is at most ϵ away from the exact values.

GREYCAT [13] aims at compressing even further the data by not limiting itself to linear models. GREYCAT also models the samples as a list of models, but these models are polynomials. The samples are read the same way.

When inserting a sample, it first checks if it fits the model. If so, then nothing needs to be done. Otherwise, unlike FLI and SWAB which directly initiate a new model, GREYCAT tries to increase the degree of the polynomial to make it fit the new sample. To do so, GREYCAT first regenerates $d + 1$ samples in the interval covered by the current model, where d is the degree of the current model. Then, a polynomial regression of degree $d + 1$ is computed on those points along the new one. If the resulting regression reports an error lower than $\frac{\epsilon}{2^{d+1}}$, then the model is kept, otherwise, the process is repeated by incrementing the degree until either a fitting model is found or a maximum degree is reached. If the maximum degree is reached, the former model is stored and a new model is initiated. The resulting model is quite compact, and thus faster to read, but at the expense of an important insertion cost.

Unlike FLI and SWAB, there can be errors higher than ϵ for the inserted samples, as the errors are not computed on raw samples but on generated ones, which may not coincide. Furthermore, the use of higher-degree polynomials makes the implementation subject to overflow: to alleviate this effect, the inserted values are normalized.

4.4   Experimental Settings

For experiments with univariate data streams—*i.e.* memory and throughput benchmarks—we set $\epsilon = 10^{-2}$. The random samples used in those experiments follow a uniform distribution in $[-1,000; 1,000]$: it is very unlikely to have two successive samples with a difference lower than ϵ, hence reflecting the worst case conditions for FLI. For experiments on location data, and unless said otherwise, we set $\epsilon = 10^{-3}$ for FLI, SWAB and GREYCAT. For GREYCAT, the maximum degree for the polynomials is set to 14. The experiments evaluating the throughput were repeated 4 times each and the average is taken as the standard deviation was low. All the other experiments are deterministic and performed once.

4.5   Implementation Details

We implemented FLI using the Flutter *Software Development Kit* (SDK) [7]. Flutter is Google's UI toolkit, based on the Dart programming language, that can be used to develop natively compiled apps for Android, iOS, web and desktop platforms (as long as the project's dependencies implement cross-compilation to all considered platforms). Our implementation includes FLI and its storage competitors. This implementation is publicly available [17].

For our experiments, we also implemented several mobile applications based on this library. To demonstrate its capability of operating across multiple environments (models, operating systems, processors, memory capacities, storage capacities), all our benchmark applications were successfully installed and executed in the devices listed in Table 1. Unless mentioned otherwise, the host device for the experiments is the Fairphone 3.

Table 1. Mobile devices used in the experiments.

Model	OS	CPU	Cores	RAM	Storage
Lenovo Moto Z	Android 8	Snapdragon 820	4	4 GB	32 GB
Fairphone 3	Android 11	Snapdragon 632	8	4 GB	64 GB
Pixel 7 Pro	Android 13	Google Tensor G2	8	12 GB	128 GB
iPhone 12	iOS 15.1.1	A14 Bionic	6	4 GB	64 GB
iPhone 14 Plus	iOS 16.0.1	A15 Bionic	6	6 GB	128 GB

5   Experimental Results

In this section, we evaluate our implementation of FLI on Android and iOS to show how it enables efficient data stream storage on mobile devices. We first perform several benchmarks (memory, throughput & stability), before evaluating the performance of FLI beyond location streams. Finally, we perform a *Point Of Interest* (POI) mining experiment directly on mobile devices, thus showcasing how FLI enables *in-situ* big data processing.

5.1   Memory Benchmark

As there is no temporal database (e.g. INFLUXDB), available on Android, we compare FLI's performances with SQLITE, the only database natively available on Android.

Synthetic Data. 2 identical operations are performed with SQLITE and FLI: *(i)* the incremental insertion of random samples and *(ii)* the incremental insertion of constant samples. The memory footprint of both solutions on disk is compared when storing timestamped values. As FLI models the inserted samples, random values are the worst-case scenario it can face, while inserting constant values represents the ideal one. One million samples are stored and, for every 10,000 insertion, the size of the file associated with the storage solution is saved. The experiments are done with a publicly available application [18].

Figure 6 depicts the memory footprint of both approaches. On the one hand, the size of the SQLITE file grows linearly with the number of inserted samples, no matter the nature (random or constant) of the samples. On the other hand, the FLI size grows linearly with random values, while the size is constant for constant values. In particular, for the constant values, the required size is negligible. The difference between vanilla SQLITE and FLI is explained by the way the model is stored: while SQLITE optimizes the way the raw data is stored, FLI is an in-memory stream storage solution, which naively stores coefficients in a text file. Using more efficient storage would further shrink the difference between the two. As expected, the memory footprint of a data stream storage solution outperforms the one of a vanilla SQLITE database in the case of stable values. While random and constant values are extreme cases, in practice data streams produced by ubiquitous devices exhibit a behavior between the two scenarios which allows FLI to lower the memory required to store those data streams.

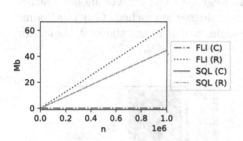

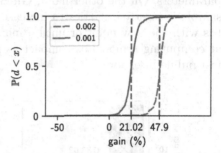

Fig. 6. Inserting $1M$ samples, random (R) or constant (C), in SQLITE and FLI.

Fig. 7. Memory gain distribution when storing CABSPOTTING with FLI.

GPS Data . We use FLI to store latitudes and longitudes of the entire CAB-SPOTTING dataset (388MB) in memory, using both $\epsilon = 10^{-3}$ and $\epsilon = 2 \times 10^{-3}$ (representing an accuracy of approximately a hundred meters). For each user, we compute the gain of memory storage as a percentage, compared to storing the raw traces. Figure 7 reports on the gain distribution as a CDF along with the average gain on the entire dataset. Most of the user traces largely benefit from using FLI, and FLI provides an overall gain of 21% (307MB) for $\epsilon = 10^{-3}$ on the entire dataset, and a gain of 47.9% (202MB) for $\epsilon = 2 \times 10^{-3}$.

Additionally, we also compare SQLITE and FLI to store the entire PRIVA-MOV dataset (7.2GB). In this context, FLI only requires 25MB (gain of 99.65%) compared to more than 5GB (gain of 30.56%) for SQLITE, despite the naive storage scheme used by FLI. Furthermore, with smartphones featuring limited RAM (cf. Table 1) and not allocating the whole of it to a single application, FLI enables loading complete datasets in memory to be processed: on mobile devices, loading the raw PRIVAMOV dataset in memory crashes the application (due to out-of-memory errors), while FLI succeeds in fitting the full dataset into RAM. This capability is particularly interesting to enable the deployment of data stream processing tasks on mobile devices that do not incur any processing overhead.

5.2   Throughput Benchmark

We compare FLI with its competitors among the temporal databases: SWAB and GREYCAT. We study the throughput of each approach in terms of IOPS. Insertion speed is computed by inserting $1M$ random samples (that is each of these solutions' worst-case scenario). For the reads, we also incrementally insert $1M$ samples before querying $10K$ random samples among the inserted ones. GREYCAT is an exception: due to its long insertion time (Sect. 4.3), we only insert $10K$ random values and those values are then queried. Our experiment is done using a publicly available application [19].

Figure 8 depicts the throughput of the approaches for sequential insertions and random reads. On the one hand, FLI drastically outperforms its competitors for the insertions: it provides a speed-up from $\times 133$ against SWAB up to $\times 3{,}505$ against GREYCAT. The insertion scheme of FLI is fast as it relies on a few parameters. On the other hand, GREYCAT relies on a costly procedure when a sample is inserted: it tries to increase the degree of the current model until it fits with the new point or until a maximum degree is reached. GREYCAT aims at computing a model as compact as possible, which is not the best choice for fast online insertions.

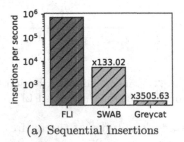

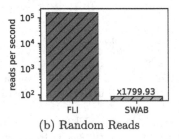

(a) Sequential Insertions   (b) Random Reads

Fig. 8. Throughput for insertions and reads using FLI, SWAB, and GREYCAT (log scale). FLI drastically outperforms its competitors for insertions and reads.

For the reads (Fig. 8b), FLI also outperforms SWAB. Our investigation reports that FLI largely benefits from its dichotomy lookup inside the time index (see Algorithm 1), compared to SWAB, which scans the list of models sequentially until the correct time index is found. SWAB reads have a complexity linear in the size of the list, while FLI has a logarithmic one. GREYCAT has the same approach as SWAB and this is why it is not represented in the results: with only $10K$ insertions instead of $1M$, its list of models is significantly smaller compared to the others, making the comparison unfair. Nevertheless, we expect GREYCAT to have a better throughput as its model list shall be shorter.

Note that those results have been obtained with the worst-case: random samples. Similarly, unfit for FLI are periodical signals, such as raw audio: our tests show a memory usage similar to random noise. Because FLI leverages linear interpolations, it performs best with signals that have a linear shape (e.g. GPS, accelerometer). We expect SWAB to store fewer models than FLI thanks to its sliding window, resulting in faster reads. However, the throughput obtained for FLI is minimal and FLI is an order of magnitude faster than SWAB for insertions, so it does not make a significant difference. We can conclude that FLI is the best solution for storing large streams of data samples on mobile devices.

5.3   Stability Benchmark

We further explore the capability of FLI to capture stable models that group as many data samples as possible for the longest possible durations. Figure 9 reports on the time and the number of samples covered by the models of FLI for the CABSPOTTING and PRIVAMOV datasets. One can observe that the stability of FLI depends on the density of the considered datasets. While FLI only captures at most 4 samples for 90% of the models stored in CABSPOTTING (Fig. 9a), it reaches up to 2,841 samples in the context of PRIVAMOV (Fig. 9c), which samples GPS locations at a higher frequency than CABSPOTTING. This is confirmed by Figs. 9b and 9d, which report a time coverage of 202 ms and 3,602 ms for 90% of FLI models in CABSPOTTING and PRIVAMOV, respectively. Given that PRIVAMOV is a larger dataset than CABSPOTTING (7.2 GB vs. 388 MB), one can conclude that FLI succeeds to scale with the volume of data to be stored.

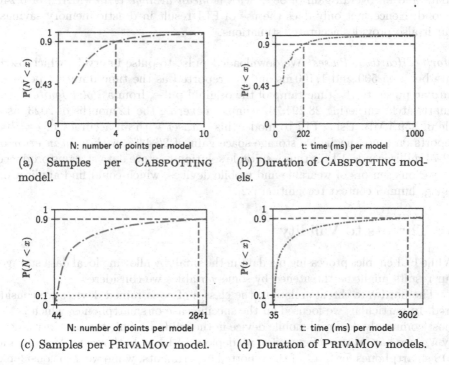

(a) Samples per CABSPOTTING model.

(b) Duration of CABSPOTTING models.

(c) Samples per PRIVAMOV model.

(d) Duration of PRIVAMOV models.

Fig. 9. Stability of the FLI models on PRIVAMOV & CABSPOTTING with $\epsilon = 10^{-3}$.

5.4   Beyond Location Streams

In this paper, FLI was mainly tested against location streams, but our proposal efficiently approximates any type of signal that varies mostly linearly: timestamps, accelerations, temperature, pressure, humidity, light, proximity, air quality, etc. This makes FLI a valuable candidate in ubiquitous contexts, as many physical quantities captured by e.g. IoT sensors have a piecewise linear behavior. To showcase different scenarios, we benchmark the storage of timestamps and heartbeat data using FLI. In both cases, we use our ϵ-tuning script to capture the most appropriate value to store the data with a reduced error.

Storing Timestamps. In all the previous experiments, the timestamps were not modeled by FLI, as we expect the user to query the time at which she is interested in the samples. However, it is straightforward to store irregular timestamps using FLI: we store couples (i, t_i) with t_i being the ith inserted timestamp. The nature of the timestamps makes them a good candidate for modeling, as insertion rates are generally fixed, or vary linearly. To assess the efficiency of FLI for storing timestamps, we stored all the timestamps of the **user 1** of the PRIVA-MOV dataset with $\epsilon = 1$—*i.e.*, we tolerate an error of one second per estimate. The 4,341,716 timestamps were stored using 26,862 models for a total of 80,592 floats and an overall gain of 98%, with a *mean average error* (MAE) of 0.246 second. Hence, not only does the use of FLI result in drastic memory savings, but it also provides accurate estimations.

Storing Heartbeat Pulses. We downloaded pulse-to-pulse intervals, which oscillate between 500 and 1,100 ms and are reported as the time duration between cardiac pulses to the timestamp of the original pulse, from a *Polar Ignite 2* [16] smartwatch, gathering 28,294,762 samples covering the 12 months of 2023, as a file of 259.1 MB. Using FLI to model this dataset with an accuracy of $\epsilon = 100$ reports on a non-negligible storage space gain of 26.44%, with a *mean error* of 22.74 milliseconds. FLI is thus a suitable solution to store data streams produced by various sensors of wearable and mobile devices, which could find application in e.g. human context recognition [22].

6   Threats to Validity

While FLI enables processing big data in the small by allowing local data storage, our results might be threatened by some variables we considered.

The hardware threats relate to the classes of constrained devices we considered. In particular, we focused on the specific case of smartphones, which is the most commonly deployed mobile device in the wild. To limit the bias introduced by a given hardware configuration, we deployed FLI on both recent Android and iOS smartphones for most of the reported experiments, while we also considered the impact of hardware configurations on the reported performances.

Another potential bias relates to the mobility datasets we considered in the context of this paper. To limit this threat, we evaluated our solutions on two established mobility datasets, CABSPOTTING and PRIVAMOV, which exhibit different characteristics. Yet, we could further explore the impact of these characteristics (sampling frequency, number of participants, duration and scales of the mobility traces). Beyond mobility datasets, we could consider the evaluation of other IoT data streams, such as air quality metrics, to assess the capability of FLI to handle a wide diversity of data streams. To mitigate this threat, we reported on the storage of timestamps and heartbeats in addition to 2-dimensional locations.

Although FLI increases storage capacity through data modeling, it might still reach the storage limit of its host device if using a constant ϵ parameter (which drives the compression rate). To address this issue, we could dynamically adapt data compression to fit a storage size constraint. Toward this end, An *et al.* [1] propose an interesting time-aware adaptive compression rate, based on the claim that data importance varies with its age.

Our implementations of FLI may suffer from software bugs that affect the reported performances. To limit this threat, we make the code of our libraries and applications freely available to encourage the reproducibility of our results and share the implementation decisions we took as part of the current implementation.

Finally, our results might strongly depend on the parameters we pick to evaluate our contributions. While FLI performances (gain, memory footprint) vary depending on the value of the ϵ parameter, we considered a sensitive analysis of this parameter and we propose a default value $\epsilon = 10^{-3}$ that delivers a minimum memory gain that limits the modeling error.

7 Conclusion

Mobile devices are incredible producers of data streams, which are often forwarded to remote third-party services for storage and processing. This data processing pattern might be the source of privacy breaches, as the raw data may leak sensitive personal information. Furthermore, the volume of data to be processed may require huge storage capacity, from mobile devices to remote servers, and network capacity to deal with the increasing number of devices deployed in the wild.

To better deal with the deluge of sensor data streams continuously generated by ubiquitous devices, we proposed FLI that unlocks *in situ* data management strategies by enabling the storage of unbounded data streams. FLI comes as an open library that can be deployed on any mobile device to store multivariate data streams, like mobility traces, 3D accelerations, or air quality metrics.

Our extensive evaluations, based on real mobile applications available for Android and iOS, highlight that FLI drastically outperforms its competitors in terms of insertion throughput—FLI is more than 130 times faster than the traditional SWAB—and read throughput—FLI reads 1,800 times faster than SWAB. Beyond its relevant performances for mobile devices, we also show that the integration of FLI paves the way for the deployment of big data processing tasks on mobile devices, hence addressing the above privacy, network and storage issues in a single solution.

Acknowledgements. This research was supported in part by the Groupe La Poste, sponsor of the Inria Foundation, in the framework of the FedMalin Inria Challenge.

References

1. An, Y., Su, Y., Zhu, Y., Wang, J.: TVStore: automatically bounding time series storage via Time-Varying compression. In: 20th USENIX Conference on File and Storage Technologies (FAST 22), pp. 83–100. USENIX Association, Santa Clara, CA (2022). https://www.usenix.org/conference/fast22/presentation/an
2. Berlin, E., Van Laerhoven, K.: An on-line piecewise linear approximation technique for wireless sensor networks. In: IEEE Local Computer Network Conference, pp. 905–912. IEEE (2010). https://gdpr-info.eu
3. Binder, S.: Drift library (2019). https://pub.dev/packages/drift. Accessed 21 Apr 2024
4. Blalock, D., Madden, S., Guttag, J.: Sprintz: time series compression for the internet of things. Proc. ACM Interact. Mobile Wearable Ubiquit. Technol. **2**(3), 1–23 (2018). https://doi.org/10.1145/3264903
5. Dollinger, V., Junginger, M.: Objectbox database (2014). https://objectbox.io. Accessed 21 Apr 2024
6. Galakatos, A., Markovitch, M., Binnig, C., Fonseca, R., Kraska, T.: Fiting-tree: a data-aware index structure. In: Proceedings of the 2019 International Conference on Management of Data, pp. 1189–1206 (2019)
7. Google: Flutter framework (2018). https://flutter.dev/. Accessed 21 Apr 2024
8. Grützmacher, F., Beichler, B., Hein, A., Kirste, T., Haubelt, C.: Time and memory efficient online piecewise linear approximation of sensor signals. Sensors **18**(6), 1672 (2018)
9. Inc, T.: Timescale database (2018). https://www.timescale.com. Accessed 21 Apr 2024
10. InfluxData: Influxdb (2013). https://www.influxdata.com/products/influxdb-overview/. Accessed 21 Apr 2024
11. Keogh, E., Chu, S., Hart, D., Pazzani, M.: An online algorithm for segmenting time series. In: Proceedings 2001 IEEE International Conference on Data Mining, pp. 289–296. IEEE (2001)
12. Liu, X., Lin, Z., Wang, H.: Novel online methods for time series segmentation. IEEE Trans. Knowl. Data Eng. **20**(12), 1616–1626 (2008)
13. Moawad, A., Hartmann, T., Fouquet, F., Nain, G., Klein, J., Le Traon, Y.: Beyond discrete modeling: a continuous and efficient model for IoT. In: 2015 ACM/IEEE 18th International Conference on Model Driven Engineering Languages and Systems (MODELS), pp. 90–99. IEEE (2015)
14. Mokhtar, S.B., et al.: Priva'mov: analysing human mobility through multi-sensor datasets. In: NetMob 2017 (2017)
15. Piorkowski, M., Sarafijanovic-Djukic, N., Grossglauser, M.: Crawdad data set epfl/mobility (v. 2009-02-24) (2009)
16. Polar: Ignite 2 (2021). https://www.polar.com/en/ignite2. Accessed 21 Apr 2024

17. Raes, R., Ruas, O., Luxey-Bitri, A., Rouvoy, R.: Fast linear interpolation implementation (2024). https://archive.softwareheritage.org/browse/origin/directory/?origin_url=https://gitlab.inria.fr/Spirals/temporaldb_apps.git&path=temporaldb (2022), last accessed on April 21st, 2024 (2022), last accessed on April 21st, 2024
18. Raes, R., Ruas, O., Luxey-Bitri, A., Rouvoy, R.: Memory space benchmarking application (2022). https://archive.softwareheritage.org/browse/origin/directory/?origin_url=https://gitlab.inria.fr/Spirals/temporaldb_apps.git&path=benchmarking_memory_space. Accessed 21 Apr 2024
19. Raes, R., Ruas, O., Luxey-Bitri, A., Rouvoy, R.: Throughput benchmarking application (2022). https://archive.softwareheritage.org/browse/origin/directory/?origin_url=https://gitlab.inria.fr/Spirals/temporaldb_apps.git&path=benchmarking_throughput. Accessed 21 Apr 2024
20. Tamplin, J., Lee, A.: Firebase services (2012). https://firebase.google.com. Accessed 21 Apr 2024
21. Timescale: Building a distributed time-series database on PostgreSQL (2019). https://www.timescale.com/blog/building-a-distributed-time-series-database-on-postgresql/. Accessed 12 May 2023
22. Vaizman, Y., Ellis, K., Lanckriet, G.: Recognizing detailed human context in the wild from smartphones and smartwatches. IEEE Pervasive Comput. **16**(4), 62–74 (2017). https://doi.org/10.1109/MPRV.2017.3971131
23. Wolfson, O., Chamberlain, S., Dao, S., Jiang, L., Mendez, G.: Cost and imprecision in modeling the position of moving objects. In: Proceedings 14th International Conference on Data Engineering, pp. 588–596 (1998).https://doi.org/10.1109/ICDE.1998.655822

Mining Profitability in Bitcoin: Calculations of User-Miner Equilibria and Cost of Mining

Enrico Tedeschi[✉][iD], Øyvind Arne Moen Nohr[iD], Håvard Dagenborg[iD], and Dag Johansen[iD]

UiT The Arctic University of Norway, 9019 Tromsø, Norway
{enrico.tedeschi,oyvind.nohr,havard.dagenborg,dag.johansen}@uit.no

Abstract. This paper examines the equilibrium between user transaction fees and miner profitability within proof-of-work-based blockchains, specifically focusing on Bitcoin. We analyze the dependency of mining profit on factors such as transaction fee adjustments and operational costs, particularly electricity. By applying a multidimensional profitability model and performing a sensitivity analysis, we evaluate the potential for profit maximization through operational cost reduction versus fee increases. Our model integrates variable electricity costs, market-driven Bitcoin prices, mining hardware efficiency, network hash rate, and transaction fee elasticity. We show that mining strategies aimed at reducing electricity expenses are far more profitable than pursuing transactions with higher fees.

Keywords: Blockchain · Bitcoin · Proof-of-Work · Mining Strategies · Profitability · Electricity Cost · Distributed Computing

1 Introduction

Bitcoin [10] and its Proof-of-Work (PoW) consensus mechanism have provided a new approach for managing trust and security in distributed systems [15]. By requiring computational work to validate and log transactions, Bitcoin eliminates the need for a central authority, overcoming the scalability and decentralization issues faced by Practical Byzantine Fault Tolerance (PBFT) consensus algorithms, which require multiple rounds of broadcast communication [2,16]. Unlike PBFT, Bitcoin's security and decentralization improve as more participants join, making 51% attacks and double spending expensive and impractical. However, this heightened security leads to increased energy consumption [11] and a fluctuating transaction fee structure [3], highlighting the trade-off between operational costs and network integrity.

The transaction fee market is an intrinsic mechanism of the Bitcoin network that allows users to incentivize miners to prioritize their transactions [1,3,14]. This market-driven approach ensures that transactions with higher fees are more likely to be included in the next block, thereby facilitating faster processing times

R. Martins and M. Selimi (Eds.): DAIS 2024, LNCS 14677, pp. 62–76, 2024.
https://doi.org/10.1007/978-3-031-62638-8_5

during periods of high network congestion. However, this system raises questions regarding its long-term viability and fairness, especially considering the variable costs and profits associated with mining.

This paper investigates the balance that PoW miners need to maintain between their operational expenses and the revenue gained from transaction fees. We examine the impact of fluctuations in Bitcoin's market price, the network's hash power, and the cost of electricity on the profitability of miners, and how these factors influence their decisions on which transactions to process. Based on a study of real-world data, we propose a financially viable model for transaction selection within the Bitcoin network, assessing how reducing operational costs could affect miners' profits compared to the potential increase in transaction fees. Understanding these strategic decisions is crucial to ensuring the sustainability and efficiency of the Bitcoin system. We specifically look at the symbiotic relationship between miners and users, detailing how miners profit and what costs they incur. Our research objective is to identify an effective strategy for a miner seeking to maximize profit while considering the importance of reducing user costs, keeping transaction fees affordable, and providing fairness for users who submit an appropriate fee [14].

Our model is based on an empirical investigation of Bitcoin mining profitability, focusing on the relevant roles of electricity costs, transaction fees, and individual hash rate. Anchored by data-driven insights, we question the long-term efficacy for miners and fairness for users of the transaction fee market emerged in Bitcoin. Our analysis is based on real-world data from Bitcoin core nodes and is complemented by blockchain.com's APIs, spanning from January 2022 to June 2023. This time period captures mining operations across diverse electricity price regimes-ranging from the low costs prevalent in Qatar to the high ones of Denmark. Our research unveils critical insights into the strategic levers miners can employ to optimize profitability.

The remainder of the paper is structured as follows: Sect. 2 presents background and related work, Sect. 3 explains the revenue mechanism for miners, and Sect. 4 presents our sensitivity analysis on miners' revenues and expenses. Next, Sect. 5 presents our calculations on miners' profitability. Section 6 emphasizes the importance of optimizing electricity costs and power efficiency for miners. Section 7 concludes.

2   Background and Related Work

The combination of user transaction fees and miner profitability within PoW blockchain systems has gathered significant attention in the academic community. Researchers have explored various aspects and factors such as transaction fee or block size adjustments [5], operational costs, and implications for system scalability and sustainability [7]. Li and Liao [9] studied the impact of Bitcoin mining on the environment and the need for a socially optimal model for the Bitcoin market. They also highlight that the increased competition in Bitcoin mining leads to high environmental costs and diminishes miners' revenue. The study concludes that it is crucial to limit speculation in Bitcoin transactions. In this paper, we show that it is possible for miners to maintain high revenue while avoiding speculation and users overspending.

Hu et al. [4] argue that transaction fees are fundamental for Bitcoin security and propose a transaction pricing mechanism from the perspective of users, with the goal of including transactions with the lowest possible fee, considering the right profit for miners. Their approach uses a pricing mechanism and a probabilistic model, wherein each transaction within the mempool is characterized by its size and time tag, which serves to assess the remaining time for inclusion. This strategy resembles the one that adopts the notions of fairness and revenue, introduced in our own studies [13]. While we recognize the significance of transaction fees in sustaining Bitcoin's security, the primary goal of this paper is to mitigate the risk of overpayment.

The trade-off between pursuing individual profit through solo mining or participating in collective mining pools has also been investigated in the work of Lajeunesse and Scolnik [7]. The study explores such trade-offs by employing a Stackelberg competition model divided into two stages. In the first stage, pools act as leaders, allocating computing power to miners (the followers), while in the second stage, miners determine their power consumption and distribution. These findings suggest that the second stage holds the potential to favor Bitcoin decentralization and stability. This paper focuses on individual computational power, excluding scenarios where miners are compelled to join mining pools.

Li et al. [8] highlight the importance of transaction fees for the sustainability of the system. Their research analyzes transaction fees under the Limited maximum Priority (LMP), designed to incentivize users to offer higher fees for transaction confirmation. Li et al. also acknowledge the key role of Bitcoin price in transaction inclusion, suggest to incorporate dynamic Bitcoin prices to design an even more efficient transaction queueing rule. In our work, we conduct experiments utilizing both dynamic Bitcoin prices and fixed projections to evaluate the potential impact on miners' revenue.

To solve the problem of computation power allocation in the Bitcoin mining network, Jiang and Wu [6] propose a hierarchical distributed computation paradigm where miners can distribute their power among multiple pools. They formulate a multi-leader multi-follower Stackelberg game to study the joint utility maximization of pool operators and miners. Emphasizing the time-varying nature of Bitcoin market prices, Jiang and Wu propose modeling it as a log-normal distribution. Oscillation in such distribution affects the equilibrium achieved by operators and miners. By comparing three distinct scenarios—fixed Bitcoin market prices, a log-normal distribution with low variance, and a log-normal distribution with high variance—the study concludes that as the market price becomes more unstable, miners contribute more to pooled mining. Building on these findings, we draw attention to the significant impact of Bitcoin price fluctuations on miners' revenue. Our analysis highlights various factors that can influence outcomes beneficial for both users and miners.

Jiang and Wu [5] investigate the economic incentives driving block size decisions in Bitcoin mining. Their research provides guidelines for optimizing default block sizes to deter miner misbehavior, contributing to network security and efficiency. They conclude that to deter miners from misbehaving, a suggested block size should be 4 MB. Given the relative stability of block sizes in recent years, we do not assume an increase in block size. Instead, our analysis estimates the potential number of transactions per block based on a rough average, allowing us to explore transaction dynamics within existing constraints.

3 Revenue Mechanism

To analyze the balance between miner profitability and user costs, it is important to understand miners' revenue mechanism. Key to this is the *coinbase transaction*, the first transaction in each block, which allows miners to earn transaction fees and block rewards. However, considering only coinbase transactions simplifies the broader economic context.

As argued by Rizun [12], a miner's profit $\langle \Pi \rangle$ is the difference between their revenues $\langle V \rangle$ and their costs $\langle C \rangle$, as follows:

$$\langle \Pi \rangle = \langle V \rangle - \langle C \rangle \tag{1}$$

The cost of computing a hash value depends on the hardware in use. Given that each hash value has the costs η, a hash rate of h, and the time to mine a block is T, the overall mining cost is

$$\langle C \rangle = \eta h T \tag{2}$$

Mining revenue comes from transaction fees M and block rewards R. When calculating expected revenue, we must also consider the probability of block orphaning $\mathbb{P}_{\text{orphan}}$, which depends on a miner's hash rate h in relation to the total network hash rate H, as follows:

$$\langle V \rangle = \frac{h}{H} \left(M + R \right) \left(1 - \mathbb{P}_{\text{orphan}} \right) \tag{3}$$

Given a block-orphaning probability of $\mathbb{P}_{\text{orphan}} = 1 - \exp(-\frac{\tau}{T})$, where τ is the block propagation delay, we obtain the following formula for miner profit calculation, which takes into consideration both operational costs, revenue potential, and orphaning risk:

$$\langle \Pi \rangle = \frac{h}{H} \left(M + R \right) \times \exp\left(-\frac{\tau}{T} \right) - \eta h T \tag{4}$$

A rational miner aims to maximize their profit ($\langle \Pi \rangle$), influenced by the network's total hash rate but primarily dependent on three factors: (1) combined transaction fees and block reward ($M + R$), (2) their hashing power (h), and (3) the probability of successfully mining a block ($1 - \mathbb{P}_{\text{orphan}}$). Given the minimal impact of an individual's hash rate, which is six orders of magnitude smaller

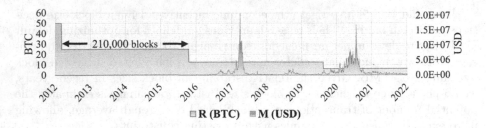

Fig. 1. Observed block rewards R and transaction fees M in the Bitcoin network from 2012 to 2022.

than the network's total hash rate-as of this writing, the total hash rate of the Bitcoin network stands at 550 million TH/s. In contrast, the hash rate provided by the most advanced and sophisticated mining rigs, such as the Bitcoin Miner S21 Hyd., is approximately 300 TH/s-and the limited control over block orphaning rates, focusing on increasing revenue through transaction fees and rewards become the primary strategy for enhancing profitability. This approach gains importance as block rewards decrease over time, underscoring transaction fees as a crucial revenue source in the long term, as can be seen in the Bitcoin network data in Fig. 1.[1] Consequently, a rational miner has three main strategies for optimizing profits:

1. Choosing transactions with higher transaction fees, which increases R;
2. Investing in additional Application Specific Integrated Circuits (ASIC) components, thereby boosting h;
3. Relocating mining operations to regions with lower electricity costs, effectively reducing the cost per hash η.

Next, we quantitatively determine the impact of each strategy on miners' profit and, consequently, on user expenses. We conduct a sensitivity analysis to examine the impact of various factors on miner profitability

4   Sensitivity Analysis

We vary the values of key parameters—such as transaction fees, hashing power, and electricity prices—to assess their influence on the overall revenue and costs of miners. We conducted experiments using partial derivatives on various variables. Specifically, we performed a sensitivity analysis on three parameters. This analysis helps us observe how changes in the values of an independent variable influence a specific dependent variable, given a particular set of assumptions. For instance, we want to assess how much the revenue changes if we keep the electricity price constant and change transaction fees, assuming a fixed Bitcoin price. Our analysis is based on the profit Eq. 4 introduced in the preceding section.

---

[1] Data source: blockchain.com.

To evaluate miners' expenses, we first determine the energy consumption E in kilowatt-hours (kWh) based on ASIC power efficiency. This enables us to calculate the cost per hash η. Energy consumption is multiplied by the electricity price to obtain the total cost. We list ASIC power efficiency η_{PE} in Joules per Terahash (J/TH), power consumption with P in Watt (W), and the hash rate h in Terahash per second (TH/s). Table 1 shows the power efficiency of most relevant mining hardware models from Bitmain.

Table 1. Power efficiency for most relevant Bitmain Antminer ASIC models based on hash rate h (TH/s) and power efficiency η_{PE} (J/TH).

Model	h (TH/s)	η_{PE} (J/TH)	Release Date
S19 Pro	110	30	May 2020
S19j Pro	100	31	Jun 2021
T19 Hydro	145	38	Oct 2022
S19 Hydro	158	34	Oct 2022
S19 XP Hyd	255	21	Oct 2022
S19j Pro+	122	28	Dec 2022
S19 Pro Hyd	177	29	Jan 2023
S19K Pro	136	24	Apr 2023
T21	190	19	Feb 2024
S21	200	17	Feb 2024
S21 Hyd	335	16	Feb 2024

We adopt the following formulas for calculating power consumption P and energy consumption E:

$$P = \eta_{PE} \times h \quad \text{and} \quad E = \frac{24P}{1000}$$

Next, we express daily profit $\langle \Pi \rangle_D$ as a function of the three variables: transaction fees (x), individual hash rate (y), and electricity price (z) as follows:

$$\langle \Pi \rangle_D(x, y, z) = \frac{y}{H}(R + x) \times \exp\left(\frac{-\tau}{T}\right) - zE \quad (5)$$

By sequentially differentiating Eq. 5 with respect to x, y, and z, we can discern the primary factors influencing the miner's profit by analyzing how the resulting equation evolves with respect to the remaining parameters. We will use this formula to demonstrate that the price of electricity is critical for a miner's profit. First, we investigate the sensitivity of miner profitability to changes in transaction fees.

4.1   Transaction Fees

To understand how profit varies with changes in transaction fees, we differentiate Eq. 5 with respect to x. This differentiation helps us analyze the sensitivity of profit to fluctuations in transaction fees while considering the influence of other parameters in the model.

$$\frac{\partial \langle \Pi \rangle_D}{\partial x}(x, y, z) = \frac{y}{H} \times \exp\left(\frac{-\tau}{T}\right) \tag{6}$$

We observe that increasing transaction fees directly augments the profit, a relationship that holds irrespective of electricity costs. Such profit is dependent on the individual hash rate h and the likelihood of successfully mining a block. Notably, miner's profit exhibits an inverse relationship with the total hash power of the network, meaning that as H increases, miners' profits tend to decrease. This relationship has a consequential effect on transaction fees. Specifically, Eq. 6 underscores the direct impact of H on transaction fees, highlighting the intricate balance between network dynamics and miners' economic incentives. Such dependency holds for individual hash rate, but does not exist between H and electricity prices.

4.2   Individual Hashing Power

To analyze the variation of profit if the individual hash rate is changed, we differentiate Eq. 5 with respect to y.

$$\frac{\partial \langle \Pi \rangle_D}{\partial y}(x, y, z) = \frac{(R + x)}{H} \times \exp\left(\frac{-\tau}{T}\right) - zE \tag{7}$$

In this context, it is evident that attempting to increase profitability solely by augmenting individual mining capacity does not translate to proportional financial returns. In fact, this multifaceted outcome is significantly influenced by external variables such as transaction fees and electricity costs, both of which bear a direct correlation to profit. Concurrently, an inverse relationship exists between profitability and the cumulative hash rate of the network, indicating that an escalation in the network's total mining capacity diminishes individual profit margins. Therefore, while increasing h is a tangible aspect of strategy, exogenous factors can have a negative impact on profitability.

4.3   Electricity Price

Analyzing the impact of electricity prices on a miner's profitability, we observe that electricity cost stands out as the most independent variable, granting miners greater control over their profitability. This is because, as shown by the derivative of Eq. 5 with respect to y, the impact of electricity prices on profit does not depend on exogenous factors, unlike transaction fees and individual hash rate considered in prior analyses. This characteristic underscores the significant

Table 2. Overview of the various mining profit variables, indicating if they are independent (✗) or interdependent (✓) of other variables.

	Variable	x	y	z
Exogenous	H	✓	✓	✗
	T	✓	✓	✗
	τ	✓	✓	✗
Endogenous	fee (x)	–	✓	✗
	$h\,(y)$	✓	–	✗
	ep (z)	✗	✓	–
	E	✗	✓	✓

degree of influence miners have over their profitability through managing electricity costs.

$$\frac{\partial \langle \Pi \rangle_D}{\partial z}(x, y, z) = -E \tag{8}$$

As captured by Eq. 8, the electricity price emerges as the only factor capable of reliably influencing profit trends, independent of external variables. This impact is directly affected by the miner's power efficiency. Hence, a rational miner would benefit from reducing electricity expenses while optimizing power efficiency to secure a definitive increase in profitability.

4.4 Parameters' Impact on Profit

We now classify variables into two categories: endogenous and exogenous, assigning different levels of influence to each based on their ability to impact profitability. Exogenous variables are those factors affecting profit but remain beyond the miners' direct control, including the total network hash rate H, block propagation delay τ, and block creation time T. In contrast, endogenous variables are within the miners' capacity to adjust and manipulate directly, provided they have access to a diverse range of transaction fees available in the mempool. Such variables include the transaction fee, individual hash rate, electricity cost, and mining power efficiency.

Table 2 lists the dependencies between various variables, highlighting the extent of control a miner has over their profitability. It becomes evident that solely increasing individual hash rate offers limited control over profit margins. In contrast, more control can be achieved through revenue-based strategies, particularly by selectively targeting transactions with higher fees. However, the minimal correlation between electricity prices and other profit-influencing factors outlines the critical role of electricity costs and mining power efficiency in managing profitability. This emphasizes the importance of optimizing operational costs to control and increase individual profit. Our claim is as follows:

Claim. To secure a stable increase in profitability, a rational miner should minimize electricity expenses and optimize power efficiency rather than selecting transactions with higher fees or increasing its hash rate.

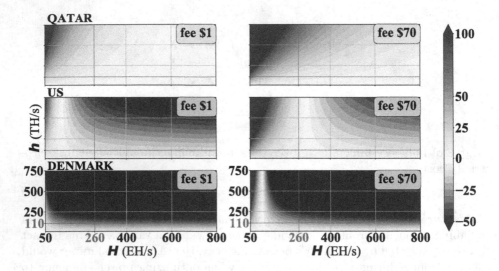

Fig. 2. Profitability of Bitcoin mining operations, including the miner's individual hashing power (TH/s) and the overall hash rate of the Bitcoin network (EH/s). The cost of electricity is considered for three countries: Qatar, the United States, and Denmark, with average fees ranging from $ 1 to $ 70. The daily profit for these miners is estimated to fluctuate between a loss of $ 50 and a gain of $ 100.

5   Miner's Profit Calculations

The initial phase of this study involved conducting profitability calculations for miners using Antminer S19 Pro ASIC. We explore the impact of varying electricity costs, categorizing them into low (Qatar at $ 0.032/kWh), medium (U.S. at $ 00.162/kWh), and high (Denmark at $ 0.469/kWh).[2] This investigation is grounded in the context of a ten-minute block creation interval, a Bitcoin valuation of $ 15,000, and transaction fees ranging between a minimum of $1 and a maximum of $ 70.

Figure 2 shows various scenarios, with each row featuring two plots showing electricity costs for the same country. The two columns represent different transaction fee averages of $ 1 and $ 70, respectively. The x-axis denotes the total hash rate of the Bitcoin Network, with the current rate at the time of the study (260 EH/s) outlined. Meanwhile, the y-axis represents individual hashing power.

---

[2] based on GlobalPetrolPrices data on electricity prices for the year 2023.

Each plot showcases daily consumption based on different combinations of individual and total Bitcoin hashing power. The figure illustrates the profitability calculations for miners operating Antminer S19 Pro across various countries. Given the assumed Bitcoin price at time of $ 15,000 and a mining reward at the time of study of ฿ 6.25, achieving profitability with low transaction fees is challenging unless electricity costs are minimized. Specifically, with a standard transaction fee of $ 1, profitable mining is practically restricted to scenarios where electricity costs are extremely low.

With the current Bitcoin hash rate, it is not possible to profit with a uniform fee of $ 1 in the U.S., and miners are advised against attempting to offset such losses by augmenting their individual hash rates, as this approach would increase their energy consumption. The most viable strategy for optimizing profitability under these conditions involve reducing electricity costs and improving mining power efficiency.

5.1 Empirical Analysis

Previous calculations made assumptions on transaction fees, bitcoin prices, and total hash power values. In contrast, our current study adopts an empirical approach, leveraging data retrieved directly from our Bitcoin core node and the Application Programming Interface (API)s offered by blockchain.com. We calculate daily profit as follows:

$$\langle \Pi \rangle_D = \langle V \rangle_D - \langle C \rangle_D \tag{9}$$

If we define g_B as the gain per block, B_D as the daily block count (simplified to 144, based on the formula: seconds in a day per T), M_μ as the day's average transaction fee, t_B as the transaction count per block (simplified to 2000), and ฿ as the current price of Bitcoin, then we can write:

$$\langle V \rangle_D = \frac{h}{H} \times g_B \times B_D \times \exp\left(\frac{-\tau}{T}\right) \qquad g_B = ฿R + t_B M_\mu$$
$$\langle C \rangle_D = z \times E$$

Figure 3 portrays the cumulative profit trajectory for a miner who switches their ASIC component according to optimal solutions determined during analysis. Data are collected from January 2022 to June 2023. The plot illustrates profit over time, assuming the miner starts mining in February 2022 and progressively upgrades their gear. Initial costs for purchasing mining components are not taken into account, as we want to focus solely on an optimal scenario driven by transaction fees and electricity prices. The graph illustrates average fee levels of $ 0.1 and $ 20 for countries with differing electricity prices. The green area highlights the zone of positive profit. Each data point represents the miner's daily profit, calculated with updated Bitcoin prices, total Bitcoin hashing power

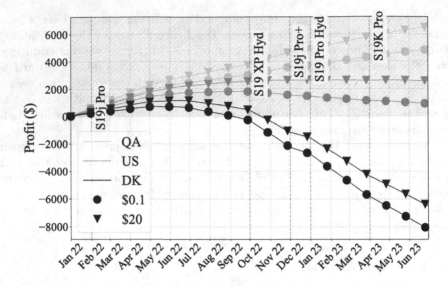

Fig. 3. Accumulated profit calculated from January 2022 to June 2023 for an individual miner utilizing different ASIC components.

and a block reward of ₿ 6.25. The study explores three scenarios characterized by different electricity costs: low (Qatar), medium (US), and high (Denmark). For each scenario, daily profits were computed with varying transaction fees.

A key insight from the analysis is the intuitive advantage of selecting a higher average transaction fee of $ 20 per transaction, the long-term profitability analysis reveals that a miner in the US, confronted with higher electricity costs would ultimately gain less compared to a miner in Qatar, who opts for a lower transaction fee of $ 0.1 per transaction. This outcome underscores the importance of electricity costs in mining profitability and suggests that strategic decisions regarding location and electricity pricing can outweigh the benefits derived from transaction fee optimization. Furthermore, if we consider the US scenario, it becomes evident that prioritizing the selection of a more suitable ASIC component outweighs the impact of transaction fees.

5.2 Bitcoin Price Variations

Additionally, we examine the sensitivity of miner profitability to variations in the Bitcoin price with two experiments in the shorter time frame from February 2022 to April 2023. Figure 4 shows cumulative profit with a Bitcoin reward of ₿ 3.125 (equivalent to the current reward) and a fixed Bitcoin price of $ 100,000. The results indicate that miners are likely to profit from mining, experiencing losses only with exceptionally high electricity prices or utilizing more powerful ASIC components if they are not energy efficient (the red area in the plot indicates a loss). The greatest profit margins are observed when electricity prices are lower, as evidenced by the gray area, which portrays the profit disparities between mining in Denmark with an average fee of $ 20 or mining in Qatar with an average fee of $ 0.1.

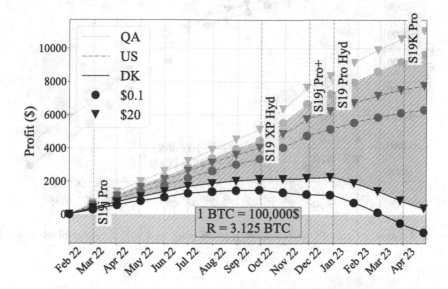

Fig. 4. Accumulated profit with a fixed Bitcoin price of $ 100,000 and a block reward of ฿ 3.125.

Figure 5 shows the potential impact of a drop in Bitcoin price to $ 10,000. Profitability is severely compromised, and the only viable option for profit is to mine with low energy consumption and high transaction fees (green area). Significant changes in transaction fees can increase yearly profit by approximately $ 1,000, while adjustments in power consumption can lead to changes that are an order of magnitude larger (grey area). This can result in a difference of nearly $ 10,000 in revenue or loss.

6   Discussion

This paper highlights the necessity for Bitcoin miners to adopt a holistic approach to profitability, considering not only the potential revenue from transaction fees and rewards but also the operational expenses, with electricity cost being a primary factor.

In regions with high electricity costs, picking high-fee transactions before lower-paying ones does not on its own guarantee sustainable profits. Consequently, the current fee market may inadvertently favor miners in geographical regions with lower electricity costs, potentially centralizing mining operations in these areas. Unpredictable transaction costs, especially during peak periods,

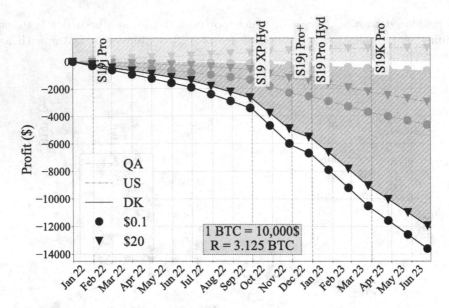

Fig. 5. Accumulated profit with a fixed Bitcoin price of $ 10,000 and a block reward of ₿ 3.125.

compel users to pay higher fees for timely processing. This could deter smaller transactions and limit the accessibility and adoption of Bitcoin. Hence, we need to consider alternative models that offer more predictable and equitable transaction fees while also encouraging decentralized mining operations.

One approach for managing transaction costs would be to standardize transaction fees or implement a dynamic fee adjustment mechanism that takes into account the average global electricity cost, thereby leveling the playing field for miners, irrespective of their location.

Incentivizing mining in regions with renewable energy sources could also reduce the overall environmental impact of Bitcoin mining and make lower transaction fees viable, benefiting both miners and users. Such a shift would require a collaborative effort among stakeholders in the Bitcoin ecosystem to redefine the parameters that govern transaction fees and mining rewards. Reflecting on the transaction fee market in light of our findings invites a broader conversation about the principles that should guide the Bitcoin network's evolution. It challenges us to envision a system that not only ensures the security and efficiency of the blockchain but also promotes sustainability.

7   Conclusion

This paper presents an empirical investigation of mining profitability in the Bitcoin system based on real-world data. We show that reductions in electricity costs significantly outweigh the marginal gains achievable through the selection of higher transaction fees or boosting individual hash rates. This is particularly evident from the comparative profitability analysis between miners in regions with divergent electricity pricing structures. Mining strategies aimed at reducing electricity expenses are far more effective in boosting long-term profitability than the pursuit of higher fee transactions or increases in mining capacity. This insight supports our earlier claim and serves as a practical guidance for miners striving to optimize their operations in the competitive and complex landscape of Bitcoin mining, especially in regions with significant electricity expenses.

References

1. Basu, S., Easley, D., O'Hara, M., Sirer, E.G.: StableFees: a predictable fee market for cryptocurrencie. SSRN Electron. J. (2019). https://doi.org/10.2139/ssrn.3318327
2. Castro, M., Liskov, B.: Practical byzantine fault tolerance and proactive recovery. ACM Trans. Comput. Syst. **20**(4), 398–461 (2002)
3. Easley, D., O'Hara, M., Basu, S.: From mining to markets: the evolution of bitcoin transaction fees. J. Financ. Econ. **134**(1), 91–109 (2019). https://doi.org/10.1016/j.jfineco.2019.03.004
4. Hu, Q., Nigam, Y., Wang, Z., Wang, Y., Xiao, Y.: A correlated equilibrium based transaction pricing mechanism in blockchain. In: 2020 IEEE International Conference on Blockchain and Cryptocurrency (ICBC), pp. 1–7. IEEE (2020)
5. Jiang, S., Wu, J.: Bitcoin mining with transaction fees: a game on the block size. In: 2019 IEEE International Conference on Blockchain (Blockchain), pp. 107–115. IEEE (2019)
6. Jiang, S., Wu, J.: On game-theoretic computation power diversification in the bitcoin mining network. In: 2021 IEEE Conference on Communications and Network Security (CNS), pp. 83–91. IEEE (2021)
7. Lajeunesse, D., Scolnik, H.D.: A cooperative optimal mining model for bitcoin. In: 2021 3rd Conference on Blockchain Research & Applications for Innovative Networks and Services (BRAINS), pp. 209–216. IEEE (2021)
8. Li, J., Yuan, Y., Wang, F.Y.: Bitcoin fee decisions in transaction confirmation queueing games under limited multi-priority rule. In: 2019 IEEE International Conference on Service Operations and Logistics, and Informatics (SOLI), pp. 134–139. IEEE (2019)
9. Li, Z., Liao, Q.: Toward socially optimal bitcoin mining. In: 2018 5th International Conference on Information Science and Control Engineering (ICISCE), pp. 582–586. IEEE (2018)
10. Nakamoto, S.: Bitcoin: A Peer-to-peer Electronic Cash System. Decentralized Business Review, p. 21260 (2008)
11. O'Dwyer, K.J., Malone, D.: Bitcoin mining and its energy footprint. In: 25th IET Irish Signals & Systems Conference 2014 and 2014 China-Ireland International Conference on Information and Communications Technologies (ISSC 2014/CIICT 2014), pp. 280–285 (2014)
12. Rizun, P.R.: A transaction fee market exists without a block size limit. Block Size Limit Debate Working Paper pp. 2327–4697 (2015)
13. Tedeschi, E.: Predictive Modeling for Fair and Efficient Transaction Inclusion in Proof-of-Work Blockchain Systems. Ph. D. thesis, UIT The Arctic University of Norway (2023)

14. Tedeschi, E., Nordmo, T.A.S., Johansen, D., Johansen, H.D.: On optimizing transaction fees in bitcoin using AI: investigation on miners inclusion pattern. ACM Trans. Internet Technol. **22**(3), 1–28 (2022). https://doi.org/10.1145/3528669
15. Tschorsch, F., Scheuermann, B.: Bitcoin and beyond: a technical survey on decentralized digital currencies. IEEE Commun. Surv. Tutorials **18**(3), 2084–2123 (2016)
16. Yin, M., Malkhi, D., Reiter, M.K., Gueta, G.G., Abraham, I.: HotStuff: BFT consensus with linearity and responsiveness. In: Proceedings of the 2019 ACM Symposium on Principles of Distributed Computing, pp. 347–356 (2019)

Author Index

© IFIP International Federation for Information Processing 2024
R. Martins and M. Selimi (Eds.): DAIS 2024, LNCS 14677, p. 77, 2024.
https://doi.org/10.1007/978-3-031-62638-8

Printed in the United States
by Baker & Taylor Publisher Services